S0-BDM-826

5-22-84

the GROWING POWER of FAITH

How to Increase YOUR Faith

by

Roxanne Brant

Mustard Seed Press
P.O. Box 1000
O'Brien, Florida 32071

WESTGATE CHAPEL
22901 Edmonds Way
Edmonds, WA 98020
(206) 775-2776

Unless otherwise indicated, all Scripture quotations in this volume are from the *King James Version* of the Bible.

ISBN 0-89274-174-0
Copyright © 1980 by Roxanne Brant
Printed in the United States of America
All Right Reserved

To the
Essenburg Family
of
Holland, Michigan
with my best love.

Through their love and friendship,
my life has been enriched,
my ministry strengthened and increased.

Contents

Foreword

Could this book change your life? Yes.

If you will read it with an open heart, there is a message here that the body of Christ needs to learn. Faith **grows! Growing faith** is a process. It takes time and effort. *Faith cometh by hearing, and hearing by the word of God.* After it comes, it needs to be nurtured.

The Growing Power of Faith is written in a simple style, easy to understand. Read it. Study it. Learn from it. It will be profitable for you and for your life.

Buddy Harrison

1

The Law of Growth

A Directive From Jesus

Jesus recently awakened me during the night and said, "Roxanne, I want you to write a book about the growth of faith." His words were warm, electric, and firm. He continued to speak to me, saying, *"Roxanne, my purpose is that My people begin to understand more about the GROWTH of faith.* Up to the present time, they have been taught much about the other triumphs and characteristics of faith, faith's operations and results. During the past several years, I have taught you much about the growth of faith. I want you to share what I have taught you with My people. *I want you to write a book about the growth of faith."*

I could see how Jesus' words were true, even in my own ministry. I had ministered more on the triumphs and characteristics of faith, teaching more about the fact that faith sees, speaks, acts, fights, perseveres, and receives from God than about the fact that faith grows.

Some Basic Principles

There are two basic and balancing facts about faith that you should understand before considering the growth of faith. The *first* fact is this: When you receive Jesus Christ as your Savior, you are born anew in your spirit. At that time, you receive His faith in seed form (Gal. 2:20). You receive all the faith that you will ever need to believe God's Word, to act upon it, and to please Him.

The *second* and balancing fact about faith is this: Although you receive enough faith at conversion to believe God's Word, to act on it, and to please Him, *the deposit of faith* which God places within you is *a faith that grows.*

Just like a muscle, faith that is constantly nurtured and exercised will increase in strength and power; this is a very important fact. And an equally important fact to understand is that *we* are the ones who use God's grace to make our faith grow. **We build our own faith.**

Like any great force, faith works by laws or principles; and the law of growth is one of these laws or principles. There are laws we can follow to make our faith grow — laws that are just as concrete as the laws we follow to make our vegetables or trees grow. The more our faith increases, the more life-giving force will be released by God into our human situations and lives to heal, deliver, change, direct, and empower us and others.

It is also very important for you to understand that there are different *strengths, levels,* or *amounts* of faith. Jesus clearly taught this, and we can see this in the natural realm. *Great* faith can move mountains that little faith can't budge, just as a truck with a V-8 engine can pull greater loads over the mountains than a truck with a V-6 engine can.

According to this same principle, we must learn to exercise faith for God to provide a little amount, such as $500 each month, before we can exercise great faith for Him to provide $50,000 each month, as some of the larger ministries require. This principle not only holds true for receiving God's material provision, but also for receiving from God in every way. You have to know how to exercise enough faith for healing a migraine headache before you can exercise enough faith for the healing of deaf ears or blind eyes. In the natural realm, for example, if a bulldozer doesn't have enough power to push over a small pine tree, how will it have the power to root out a huge oak tree?

Faith is a force that we can build up in our lives. The amount of faith we have after a period of time, and whether that faith grows quickly or slowly, is up to us. *More faith* can free God to work in lavish abundance in our lives while *less faith* can limit His working — not only in our lives, but in the lives of those around us. With *more* faith, we can move mountains; with *less* faith, we can move only hills. It is our responsibility to understand that there are different levels of faith and to understand how the laws of faith work. We must know our part in the nurture and care of the seed of faith — how to make it increase and help it grow to its full potential.

In talking about faith, Jesus said, *When it is sown, it GROWETH UP, and becometh greater than all herbs, and shooteth out great branches; so that the fowls of the air may lodge under the shadow of it* (Mark 4:32). Pictured as a mustard seed, *faith has a small beginning when God plants it in our hearts.* When it has grown up, however, it can fulfill its powerful, creative role, and destiny in our lives. If it is to become that huge tree of faith in our lives — the powerful, effective force we want it to be — we must faithfully feed and nurture it. Much confusion would disappear if people realized that great faith doesn't come overnight any more than a tree or bush grows overnight. *After the PLANTING of faith, there must be a PERIOD OF GROWTH before we see a FULL HARVEST of faith's results in our lives.*

Jesus not only talked about the growth of faith, but He also spoke of different *amounts* or *levels* of faith. In Mark 4:40, for example, He said the disciples had *no* faith. In Matthew 14:31, He indicated that Peter wasn't able to continue walking on the water because he had *little* faith. Yet, of two gentiles, Jesus declared He found in them *great* faith. (Matt. 8:10 and 15:28.)

Different amounts of faith release different amounts of God's power and blessing into our lives, and through our lives to others. The equation is very simple: *More faith releases more power and blessing in our lives; less faith releases less power and blessing in our lives.* We don't begin the Christian life with great faith, but rather with a seed of Jesus' faith — *the faith of the Son of God, who loved me, and gave himself for me* (Gal. 2:20). That seed has MULTIPLYING POTENTIAL which, when patiently nurtured, will produce great faith in us.

If you desire to have the great faith that will work creative miracles and move mountains for the glory of God, then you need to understand this principle thoroughly. **There is a period of growth between God's planting the seed of faith in our hearts and our being able to reap the harvest of mighty miracles.** If you have a firm knowledge of the principles involved in how to make your faith grow, you won't be easily discouraged. Instead, you will be encouraged as you see the small, but daily, increase of your faith as you walk in communion and fellowship with our Lord.

Before I talk more about the growth of faith, however, I want to emphasize the importance of faith in the Christian life and the importance of understanding faith's principles, which you should build into your life.

The Importance of Faith

God's Word is very emphatic about the importance of faith. In fact, the Scriptures declare four times that *the just shall live by faith* (Hab. 2:4; Rom. 1:17; Gal. 3:11; Heb. 10:38). The Word of God makes clear that the *commencement, continuation,* and *completion* of the Christian life is *by faith.* **The only way we can progress in the Christian life is by faith.**

In spite of this, most people feel that if they are good, they will please God. God clearly says, however, that it is **not** our goodness that pleases Him, but **our faith,** for *without faith it is impossible to please God* (Heb. 11:6). God is a faith God who established the universe on faith principles. **All of His promises and all that a Christian can ever hope to accomplish, attain, or become cannot be realized apart from faith.**

Consider the place of faith in the Christian experience.

By faith, we are:
    saved (Acts 16:31; Eph. 2:8; Rom. 5:1).
    sanctified (Acts 15:9; 26:18).

kept (1 Pet. 1:5; Rom. 11:20; 2 Cor. 1:24).
healed (James 5:15; 1 Pet. 2:24; Acts 14:9).
baptized in the Holy Spirit (Gal. 3:5, 13, 14).
By faith, we:
receive God's material provision (Phil. 4:19).
walk (2 Cor. 5:7).
surmount difficulties (Rom. 4:18-21; Heb 11:17-27; Mark 9:23).
live (Rom. 1:17).
please God (Heb. 11:6).
have access to God (Rom. 5:2; Eph. 3:12).
overcome Satan (1 John 4:4; 5:4, 5; Rev. 12:11).
stand in victory (1 John 5:4, 5; 2 Cor. 1:24).
Through faith, God uses us to **obtain help for others and bless them** (John 7:38; Mark 2:3-5; Acts 27:24).

Certainly these scriptures reveal the importance of faith, but they reveal something else, too. God doesn't reward us or respond to us on the basis of our human goodness but according to our faith. **It is faith that moves the hand of God.**

Faith, Not Goodness, Moves God's Hand

Wherever I travel across the country, speaking in churches and auditoriums, I am consistently confronted by two basic misconceptions Christians have which keep them from receiving God's blessings.

The *first misconception* I have found is that **people are still believing God will heal them because they are good.** As I have already shown, however, it is faith that causes God to heal you.

This was impressed upon me very deeply once as I held a series of meetings in New England, not far from where I had lived before moving to Florida. Many of my life-long friends, who had been converted under my ministry, came to those services. I was not aware they were coming that particular evening until I looked down from the pulpit to see several pews in the front of the church filled with these good friends. Looking down on them, I thought how precious they were to me. What loving people they were, and how good it was to see them again! They were some of the best people I knew, so loving and so kind. They were not very faith-filled, however.

After the healing service, we noted the healings, heard the testimonies, and gave glory to the Lord. It was obvious that the Lord had not healed even one of my friends; yet He healed so many other people that night. After I spent time with my friends and returned to the hotel, I talked with the Lord.

"Jesus, You skipped over the nicest people tonight — some of the best, most loving people I know — my friends seated in the front pews. Lord, You healed people all over the church — even some of the most unpleasant, difficult, and unsanctified people on the back pews of that church — but You completely passed over my friends. I don't understand that, and it bothers me."

The Lord said, "Roxanne, your friends are nice and they are loving, but they have very little faith. The difficult and unpleasant people who were seated in the back of the church aren't nice by your standards, but they are filled with faith. *Faith, not human goodness, moves My hand.*"

I will never forget the illumination that came with those words. **God responds to us according to our faith;** while in the human realm, we tend to respond to people according to their goodness and capabilities. If we had to choose which people we would heal, we would heal those who are *loving* and *good* — the upright people who are so considerate and helpful to others. But that isn't the way God does it! **He heals people who are filled with faith. It is faith, not human goodness, that moves His hand!** (Heb. 11:6.)

God Is Waiting For YOU To Move

The *second misconception* that needs to be corrected is the notion that **God responds to you according to your need.** People are waiting for God to see their need, then move according to their need and heal them.

Christians who need healing are sitting in their church pews every week, all across America, still thinking things like, "God will see my thyroid problem if I wait long enough, and He will move to meet my need. All I have to do is wait, and God will see my need and move to meet it." This is religious thinking! It is just plain wrong! The tense is wrong; therefore, it is unscriptural.

God won't move to meet your need because **He has already moved.** He has already met every need you will have — tomorrow, the next day, and the next. **He met it 2,000 years ago in Jesus Christ on the cross.** Today, He is waiting for you to realize that. He is waiting for you to believe and act by faith on His Word that He has already moved to meet your need in Christ. **Your faith is the key that will unlock God's provision and bring that provision or answer into your life by the power of His Spirit — today.**

We desperately need to have our minds renewed by the Word of God (Rom. 12:2.) We need to stop thinking the way this world thinks and **begin thinking the way God thinks.** Then we will begin to understand His ways and walk in them. Then we will begin to understand His wisdom and act according to His laws, not against them.

The Planting of Faith: God's Initial Deposit Is Given, Dealt, and Comes

As you think about *how* faith grows, it is apparent that it *first* has to have a beginning or planting in your heart. How, then, does faith initially come to you?

The Bible says that first you turn from your sins to Jesus Christ and say, "Jesus, come into my life and forgive all my sins. I believe that You died on the cross and took the punishment for my sins. I believe that You are the Son of God and my Savior" (Rom. 10:9, 10). At that point, God forgives your sins and plants Jesus' nature — His life and His faith — into your innermost being, your heart. There is a definite planting of faith — the faith of Jesus Christ — although in *seed form,* into you — the believer — at the time of conversion.

I want to make clear just what kind of faith I am talking about so there will be no confusion in your mind. There is an extraordinary kind of faith referred to in 1 Corinthians 12, called "the gift of faith," which

God gives to a person to bring a needed miracle. However, the "gift of faith" is temporary; it doesn't stay with you, but comes and then goes.

The kind of faith I am talking about is *the seed of faith* that God plants in your spirit at conversion. In theology, we call it "saving faith." It is the kind of faith we use or exercise to live and please God every day of our lives. This "saving faith" is *supernatural;* it is *His* faith, the faith of Jesus, Who loved us so much that He gave Himself for us. (Gal. 2:20.) That faith isn't something you had before you were saved; God gave it to you at the time of your conversion to Christ.

So many people struggle, trying to make their faith grow. They worry about their faith, but they don't need to do so. I tell Christians, "Have faith in the faith within you because it is God's faith, His supernatural faith, that dwells and works within you. The faith of Jesus has been planted in you; and it is the same faith by which Jesus Christ overcame the world. The devil couldn't defeat it! Hell couldn't hold it! The grave couldn't contain it! It is *a tested faith,* more powerful than anything in this universe. It is *the faith of God, a supernatural faith;* **but** it is up to **you** to make it grow!"

When God plants His faith in our hearts, He says that it is *given*. Ephesians 2:8, 9 states: *For by grace are ye saved through faith; and that not of yourselves: it is the **gift** of God: not of works, lest any man should boast.*

God clearly tells us that the seed of faith, sometimes called "saving or general faith," is a gift of His grace. The Bible also speaks of that faith as being "dealt," which is just another word for "given." In Romans 12:3 Paul was inspired to write:

> *For I say, through the grace given unto me, to every man that is among you, not to think of himself more highly than he ought to think; but to think soberly, according as God hath **dealt** to every man the measure of faith.*

In another place, Paul describes the planting of faith this way: *So then faith cometh by hearing, and hearing by the word of God* (Rom. 10:17).

There are three words God uses to tell us about how we receive His faith: *gift, dealt, cometh.* All convey the fact that faith is *given* to us. Faith doesn't come, then, by struggling or by begging God; it simply comes by hearing God's Word, for God's Words contain faith.

Simply stated then: *Coffee comes in coffee cups, and faith comes in the Word of God.* For example, when you go into a restaurant and say, "I would like a cup of coffee, please," you know that coffee will come in a cup or container. It will not be poured into your hands. Just as coffee comes in a container, faith too comes in a container: *Faith comes packaged or wrapped in God's Word.* We need to remember that when we read the Bible, we are getting more than just information; we are also receiving **life** and **faith** through God's Words. Therefore, if we need faith for healing, for finances, for protection, for guidance, or for anything else, all we have to do is read the Word of God and hear it.

In studying the original Greek, we find that words which have been translated *word* in our English Bible are actually two Greek words: *rhema* and *logos*. The word *rhema* refers to the Spirit-anointed portion of God's Word which He speaks into your spirit, while the word *logos* refers to the total revelation of God in the Bible.

Because the Scriptures say, *faith cometh by hearing, and hearing by the word* (rhema) *of God* (Rom. 10:17), some people have said that we need a *rhema* word from God for faith to come. Therefore, if those people see a person in a wheelchair who needs healing, but they do not receive the *rhema* Word of God to produce faith within them for the healing of that sick person, they will not pray. They simply leave the sick person without praying.

I want to talk about the above conception and share what Jesus taught me about the difference between the *rhema* and the *logos* Word of God in regard to producing faith within our hearts.

Hatched and Unhatched

As I was praying one evening, Jesus spoke two different words to me regarding the production of faith: *hatched* and *unhatched*.

Jesus said, "Roxanne, it is true that My *rhema* words produce faith in your heart. But if you do not receive a *rhema* word from Me, you simply take My *logos* word, or promise, into your mouth and heart. Meditate on it, speak it forth, and **hatch it.**"

He continued, "The difference between My *rhema* words and My *logos* words in producing faith is that the *rhema* words come to you *hatched* with faith; My *rhema* words are already *hatched* or alive with faith. However, My *logos* words come to you *unhatched*. Though My *logos* words are powerful and filled with life (Heb. 4:12), you need to put them through a process before they will produce faith in you. You need to *hatch* them. This process of *hatching* is simple."

(Here Jesus brought to my remembrance an outline I had heard somewhere and jotted down in my "sermon notebook." I have forgotten the source or author.)

He said, "There are **four basic steps:**

1. **Investigation** — You read My Word (*logos*) and select the promises you need.

2. **Incubation** — You *hatch* My Word (*logos*) as you meditate on it and speak it forth consistently every day. Here the *logos* changes to *rhema*.

3. **Illumination** — The Holy Spirit will unveil My Word to you in a personal way, making it real and alive to you — a *rhema* Word.

4. **Impartation** — Then the Holy Spirit imparts faith into your spirit from that *rhema* Word.

"Whenever you receive a *rhema* Word, it comes to you already *hatched* and automatically produces faith in your heart. But if you do not receive a *rhema* Word and you need faith — to receive healing, a miracle of some kind, or to pray for someone in need — then take My *logos* Word and go through this process of *hatching. If My Word does not come to you hatched, then you need to take it and hatch it yourself until it produces faith in your heart."*

We can see a simple illustration of the above principle in the natural realm. Some farmers buy young chicks already hatched. Others buy fertilized eggs which they place in an incubator or under hens to go through a process of hatching (or incubation) after which young chicks will come forth. *There are two ways to obtain the same result, either buy your chicks already hatched or hatch them yourself.*

So it is with the Word of God. It either comes to you *hatched,* or you have to put it through a process of incubation and *hatch* it yourself. Either way the end result is the same — **a heart filled with productive faith.**

God will turn the logos word into a rhema word for you as you faithfully meditate on His promises and speak them forth. If you need faith for healing, read and confess the promises for healing from God's Word. If you need faith for provision, read and confess the promises for provision from God's Word. Confess them 100 or 1,000 times if you have to, and you will have much more faith after the 100th or 1,000th time than when you began speaking them forth. **Make your faith grow by choosing the promises of God for your situation, meditating on them, and speaking them forth as you act on His Word for your life.**

2

Growing Power

Faith . . . Groweth Up (Mark 4:32)

Faith is like one of your muscles. If you use faith, it increases in strength and power; but if you don't exercise it, it will become weak and ineffective.

Faith won't stay on standby. In fact, your faith can't stand still, because you live in an opposition-filled world. Since your adversary doesn't relax his opposition toward you, you can't relax your faith. However, it is comforting to know that **feeding and using your faith in the midst of that opposition makes it grow.**

Jesus emphasized the fact that faith grows, just as the kingdom or rule of God over us grows, when He spoke forth the parable of the mustard seed. He said:

> *Whereunto shall we liken the kingdom of God? or with what comparison shall we compare it?*
>
> *It is like a grain of mustard seed, which, when it is sown in the earth, is less than all the seeds that be in the earth:*
>
> *But when it is sown, it groweth up, and becometh greater than all herbs, and shooteth out great branches; so that the fowls of the air may lodge under the shadow of it* (Mark 4:30-32; see also Matt. 13:31, 32 and Luke 13:18, 19).

Just as Jesus compared faith to a mustard seed in Luke 17:6, so also in the above parable, He again compares faith — as well as the kingdom or rule of God in our hearts — to a grain of mustard seed. In this parable Jesus emphasizes that both faith and the rule of God over us are like a grain of mustard seed in certain ways.

He first teaches us that, when planted, each has a very small beginning, but a large ending or culmination in our lives.

The second point He emphasizes is that both faith and the kingdom or rule of God in our hearts, when planted, *grow up*. In other words, each has a **growing potential** within us, *but they will not automatically grow to maturity*.

In the natural realm, even though a seed has growing or multiplying potential, if we wish it to grow, we must not only plant it, but water it, cultivate it, and guard it from weeds which would choke it. When cared for and properly nurtured, the *potential* growing power in the mustard seed is amazing. That tiny seed grows into a 12-foot plant. In Jesus' day, throughout Israel, the contrast between the tiny size of the mustard seed and the great size of the plant it finally produced in its full growth was proverbial.

Jesus said of the mustard seed, *When it is sown, it groweth up* . . . . In the same way, both faith and the rule of God over us have a tiny beginning in our lives, but a great and powerful culmination. Why? Because, when planted, they *grow up*. Remember, Jesus said that the seed first had to be planted; then over a period of time, it would *grow up*.

It is important to see that **a period of time is required for the mustard seed to reach maturity.** The law of growth is a spiritual law, and growth is a process. Jesus wants you to be encouraged, not discouraged, when you don't see the full rule of God or the full development of your faith manifested immediately in your life.

The fact that faith grows over a period of time, just as the kingdom or rule of God in our hearts grows over a period of time, is a truth we can easily see illustrated in our own Christian experience. For example, we first begin the Christian life with a child-like faith, by receiving Christ into our hearts. We say, "Jesus, forgive my sins. I believe You are my Savior, that You died for me on the cross. Take my life. Take all that I am. Take all that I have and use me. Jesus, I want You to be my Lord as well as my Savior." When we pray that prayer, Jesus immediately enters our lives and begins His sovereign work in us.

Contrary to what some people may think or expect, Jesus doesn't take over every bit of our lives in one minute. His total rule of us is not manifested immediately. It comes over a period of time; it is a process. That is one reason our peace increases over a period of time. Peace comes as we allow His rule in our lives to increase. Referring to Jesus' coming rule as Sovereign of all the earth, the prophet Isaiah said, *Of the increase of his government and peace there shall be no end* (Is. 9:7). The principle that *Christ's increased government* or rule over us brings *increased peace* into our lives over a period of time is a spiritual truth.

Let me illustrate how the rule of God might increase in your life. When you received Jesus as your Savior, you were **instantly** made a new creation in your spirit, perfect in the sight of God. At that moment you were robed in His righteousness. (2 Cor. 5:17.) But that new life of Jesus Christ still has to continue moving into dominion over each area of your soul — into your mind, your emotions, and your affections. It has to change your habits and attitudes, gradually bringing them into harmony with God's perfect plan for your life. The more you allow that new life of Christ to permeate your being, the more you will think, feel, and desire the things of God. This is the process of being renewed in the spirit of your mind (Eph. 4:23), the process of being transformed by the renewing of your mind (Rom. 12:2).

A familiar analogy for this process is to compare our lives with a house. When you ask Christ into the "house" of your life, He comes into the living room area which represents the central area of your life — your human spirit. Jesus does not take over the whole "house" in one minute. He extends His dominion from the living room, or spirit area, into the other rooms which represent the soul areas of your life. **He does this as you make concrete, minute-by-minute choices to obey His Word in your attitudes, affections, emotions, habits, and appetites.**

Jesus wants to extend His dominion or rule over **your** life and bring it into **His** order, letting it reflect His beauty in every room of your soul area. He wants to extend His dominion into the den, kitchen, bedroom, garage, cellar, and all other areas of your "house." For example, let's say He wants to extend His lordship into the den area of your life. One day you find yourself in the den watching television and Jesus gently nudges you to pray and intercede for a friend. If you say to Him, "Lord, wait until the commercial and then I'll pray," you know that He is not yet Lord of the "den" in your life. And He will not be Lord of your "den" until you become obedient to His nudges, His Word. It is only when you obey Jesus, turn off the television, and pray for a friend as the Holy Spirit leads you to intercede, that Jesus becomes Lord in the "den" of your life.

The moment you obey Jesus, giving Him precedence over the television set, and He becomes Lord of your "den," then He can begin working in your heart that He might exercise dominion in another area — your appetites. In the area of the kitchen, just as you are about to sit down to a juicy steak, Jesus might ask you to fast and pray. Perhaps you tell Him that you will fast tomorrow when your menu at home calls for meatloaf. If so, then He isn't Lord of your "kitchen." After a time, you may place a higher priority on intercession than on a meal the Holy Spirit asks you to forfeit, possibly to pray for someone's healing. When you reach that place, then you can let Jesus become Lord in another area of your life.

When you awaken at three in the morning and feel a gentle nudge of the Holy Spirit to intercede in prayer, you can know that Jesus is asking to be made Lord of your "bedroom," too. When you are willing to be obedient and sacrifice sleep to "watch and pray" for a night if He asks you to do so, you are allowing Jesus to be Lord of another room in the house of your life.

We can see, then, how **Jesus' rule increases and continues to grow or extend over the various areas of our lives as we make concrete choices to do His will.**

The growth of Jesus' rule over us is a process that takes time. Jesus is telling this truth to us in the parable of Mark 4:30-32. Also, He is saying that the rule of God in our lives is not only a process, but it has a small beginning and a great culmination. It continues to grow throughout our being while we are living on this earth.

The growth of faith in our lives is just like the growth of God's rule in our lives. That is the teaching of Jesus. Faith, like a tiny mustard seed, has a small beginning; but, in time, as it is nurtured, that seed will sprout, grow, and fulfill a powerful destiny in our lives. Faith *can* become a powerful force that will move mountains for us and for others.

Since we see that faith can grow, the first logical question to ask is: How much potential is in the seed? How high will it grow? Jesus was talking about the mustard seed. As mentioned previously, it is a plant — not actually a tree — which most Bible scholars think grew to be about twelve feet tall under favorable conditions. Jesus wanted the people He taught to understand the principle of growth, so He used this vivid example, demonstrating what a difference there is between the tiny size of the mustard seed and the great twelve-foot plant it finally produces.

We really should not be surprised to discover the fact that faith grows, for as we read God's Word, we find that **the law of growth touches everything in the spiritual realm.** It is an all-pervasive law of God that affects **every** area of our Christian lives. **We are to grow:**

in faith (2 Thess. 1:3).

in love (1 Thess. 3:12).

in the knowledge of God (Col 1:10).

in grace (2 Pet. 3:18).

Peace and mercy should also be multiplied to us (Jude 2); and as we walk with God and give bountifully for the propagation of His kingdom, He will not only increase our seed for sowing, but also increase the harvest of our fruits of righteousness. (2 Cor. 9:10.) The law of growth is, therefore, a spiritual law of God. As we look to Him and obey His Word in every area of our lives, we will increase with the increase of God. (Col. 2:19.) Praise the Lord!

The Apostle Paul, like our Lord Jesus, spoke a great deal about faith. He wrote to the Thessalonian Christians and said:

> *We are bound to thank God always for you, brethren, as it is meet, because that your faith groweth exceedingly, and the charity of every one of you all toward each other aboundeth* (2 Thess. 1:3).

Paul gloried and rejoiced in the blessings of God manifest in his converts in Thessalonica, and one of those blessings was their **exceedingly growing faith.** On the other hand, Paul was waiting for the faith of the Corinthian Christians to grow. He wrote that he had hope that **when their faith increased,** he would be able to leave them and preach the Gospel in regions beyond

Corinth where the Gospel had not been previously preached. He wrote them of his hope saying:

> . . . *having hope, your faith is increased, that we shall be enlarged by you according to our rule abundantly,*
>
> *To preach the gospel in regions beyond you* (2 Cor. 10:15, 16).

Faith That Grows Like a Grain of Mustard Seed

The parallel passage of Scripture on the mustard seed became vividly alive after Jesus started to speak to me about the growth of faith. In Luke 17:5, 6 the apostles came to the Lord and asked Him to increase their faith:

> *And the apostles said unto the Lord, Increase our faith.*
>
> *And the Lord said, If ye had faith as a grain of mustard seed, ye might say unto this sycamine tree, Be thou plucked up by the root, and be thou planted in the sea; and it should obey you.*

The apostles desired more faith. When they came to the Lord and said to Him, "Lord, increase our faith," they requested something very practical. If you had lived during the time of the apostles and walked in their shoes, you would have had the same desire they had for increased faith. In fact, you should have that desire now.

The apostles had some faith, but they wanted more. They walked with Jesus and watched Him work hundreds of miracles among great crowds of people who were suffering. They saw hundreds of little children and thousands of people who were wracked with pain, filled with leprosy, and living with crippling diseases. They wanted to see those people freed because they loved them, because they had compassion on them. They wanted **more** faith, so that they could lay hands on more people and release **more** of God's power to help multiplied thousands of people, instead of only hundreds. Jesus had healed so many people, thousands of them, but there were many thousands more remaining who needed healing and help. Therefore, the apostles' hearts cried out just as our hearts would have cried out and still do today, *Lord, increase our faith.*

I know that faith is increased by hearing and acting on the Word of God and that is how faith comes and grows. But in some countries where I go to hold crusades in the world today, I still find myself crying out, *Lord, increase my faith!* I pray that prayer because I have compassion for people who are sick and in pain, people who need Christ.

During my first South American crusade, I prayed for more faith because I stood in front of a sea of needy people. I could see hundreds who were brought there on pallets and many who were paralyzed or crippled with arthritis and other painful diseases. These people were so poor that they didn't even have money for decent food and clothing, much less medicine. Many of them had walked for hours to come to the meeting, which was held outdoors.

As I stood before them, I felt the compassion of God rise within me and flow out to those people. That flow of God's love was so strong that it almost picked me up off my feet, but I needed more faith and I knew it. I prayed, "Lord, increase my faith so that You can work bigger miracles and heal more people tonight than ever before in my ministry." God poured out His Spirit (see 1 Cor. 12), faith abounded, and so did His miracle-working power. Hundreds of people were healed that night. During the crusade, hundreds came to receive Jesus as Lord and Savior, and God was truly glorified!

After I returned from that South American crusade, I understood so much more fully what the disciples felt when they asked Jesus to increase their faith. However, Jesus' answer to their request puzzled me until just recently. He said:

> *If ye had faith as a grain of mustard seed, ye might say to this sycamine tree, Be plucked up by the root, and be thou planted in the sea; and it should obey you* (Luke 17:6).

I never understood Jesus' answer to the apostles, but I have heard many people present their views on exactly what Jesus meant. Most people have said that *Jesus meant the apostles only needed faith the size of a grain of mustard seed to work mighty miracles. But it simply isn't true that **little faith** will work **great miracles,*** so that interpretation of Jesus' words never made sense to me.

Other people teach that Jesus was talking to the apostles about the *genuineness* or *sincerity* of their faith. These people teach that you only need sincere or genuine faith to work mighty miracles. Other people teach that you don't need great faith for mighty miracles; you only need a little bit of faith in a big God. There may be some truth in each of these ideas, but I believe they are missing the point of Jesus' teaching entirely.

First, *it simply isn't true that little faith will work great miracles*. The Bible consistently presents the principle that little faith works small miracles, while we need great faith for great miracles. It is true that *each Christian has at least a mustard seed size of faith planted within him at conversion*. Paul, the apostle, has written in Romans 12:3 that God has given to every Christian the "measure of faith." I believe this measure of faith is, therefore, the mustard seed size faith planted within the Christian at conversion.

Each Christian begins the Christian life with the same amount of faith, a mustard seed size faith or the "measure of faith." I believe that the apostles (as well as every Christian, myself included) began the Christian life with the very same size faith. It depends on how you nourish your faith as to how strong it will grow.

If mustard seed size faith — the size faith with which we all begin the Christian life — will work great miracles, **where are all the great miracles?** Where are all the blind eyes being opened? Where are all the deaf ears being unstopped? Where are all the paralyzed people being raised out of wheelchairs? Where are all the terminal cancer patients being healed? *If mustard seed size faith works great miracles, then each Christian should be working great miracles from his experience of the new birth onward, because he has been dealt the measure of faith or mustard seed size faith.*

I asked the Lord to enlighten my understanding of what He wanted me to see regarding His answer to the apostles. The first thing He emphasized to me was that *the apostles knew what they were asking for* when they asked for more faith. *They understood the laws of faith* because, before the time they requested Jesus to increase their faith, they had been sent out by Jesus to preach the kingdom of God and to heal the sick. (Luke 9.) Jesus had sent them out with this commission:

> *And as ye go, preach, saying, The kingdom of heaven is at hand.*

> *Heal the sick, cleanse the lepers, raise the dead, cast out devils* (Matt. 10:7, 8).

The apostles had gone out under Jesus' authority and power, had cleansed lepers, cast out devils, and raised the dead. They knew much about faith and how the laws of faith operate. They knew how to exercise their faith. Therefore, when they came to Jesus and asked Him to increase their faith, they knew what they were asking for.

The apostles wanted more of the same thing. Some people seem to slight the apostles and say that they did not understand their request, but if we judge from the results they had in operating by faith — healing the sick and raising the dead — we can only conclude that they knew more about faith than most of us do today. Remember also that *their request came before the resurrection of Jesus Christ.* We can be sure, however, that Jesus gave the apostles a legitimate answer to their question. His answer was direct and not evasive.

Though I did not understand His answer initially, I knew that it must contain something to reveal the increase of faith. I continued to ask Jesus for more revelation or insight on the text in Luke 17:5, 6. I kept meditating on those verses, and even checked my Greek Testament for help, but did not see anything that further illuminated the biblical text.

One day, however, as I was meditating further on Jesus' answer to the apostles, the Lord spoke these words to me: *that groweth up!* My heart began to beat very quickly. The words were warm, firm, and clear; they brought life flooding through my spirit!

Jesus continued speaking to me:

Roxanne, My answer to the apostles was, "If ye had faith . . . that groweth up . . . as a grain of mustard seed, ye might say unto this sycamine tree, Be thou plucked up by the root, and be thou planted in the sea; and it should obey you" (Luke 17:6).

Jesus' words, **that groweth up,** kept echoing in my spirit. My heart was still pounding as my mind rushed back to Mark 4:32 concerning the law of the growth of faith and the fact that when the seed of faith, the mustard seed, is sown, "it *groweth up* and becometh greater than all herbs." The Lord continued to talk to me and said:

Roxanne, I'm talking about the GROWTH of faith here also. I was telling the apostles that their faith has to grow over a period of time. I was encouraging them to see that their faith could, in time, become so powerful that, when they spoke the word of faith to even the most stubborn obstacles in life, those obstacles would not be able to resist it.

I understood very clearly that **Jesus was telling the apostles that they needed faith that grows like a grain of mustard seed.** He was talking about **the growth of faith** in that particular scripture.

I wondered then why it had taken so long for me to see what Jesus had explained so simply. *Why had I been so blind to such a simple truth?*

One thing I realized was that I had taken four years of seminary training, but had never studied the things Jesus used as examples in any practical way. For example, I knew about seeds in my mind, but had never had any practical experience with them. Theologians and scholars know so much about biblical theology, pastoral care, church administration, church history, the Hebrew and Greek languages, hermeneutics and exegesis; but they know little about planting seeds and seeing them grow.

Jesus was speaking to people who lived in a farming culture. They had farming in their veins, so to speak, as well as a great love for the land, for planting, for cultivating, and for harvesting. They took joy in these things and, therefore, quickly grasped the spiritual insight Jesus was trying to convey about the fact that *faith grows in the spiritual realm the way a grain of mustard seed grows in the natural realm.*

The Multiplying Potential of Faith

Jesus knew that His listeners understood something else about seeds. *They knew about the multiplying potential or power in a seed; therefore, they grasped the spiritual truth about the multiplying potential or multiplying power resident in the seed of faith.*

Jesus was telling the apostles that faith had a multiplying potential or multiplying power that would eventually be able to accomplish some very sizable jobs. In speaking of a black mulberry tree (the sycamine tree), the people of Jesus' day knew that its root could remain in the earth for hundreds of years, that plucking it up by the root would be an extremely difficult job. Jesus' listeners would have understood that *He was talking about faith's ability to become very powerful in their lives,* that *faith had a tremendous multiplying potential in regard to its strength* and that *it could eventually be powerful enough to move mountainous problems.*

Jesus helped His listeners to see clearly the multiplying potential in the seed of faith.

It is easy, and often very encouraging, to look back on our natural lives and see how we have grown in many areas.

We have grown physically from just over a foot, at birth, to over five or six feet in height at present.

We have grown mentally. At birth we couldn't speak or appreciate much of our world. Today, we can understand and appreciate even arts and sciences or other disciplines in the natural world. We appreciate our ability to participate in such things.

We can also look back on our spiritual lives with God and see how *we have grown spiritually.* **We grow**

spiritually as our faith grows, and faith grows in every area of our Christian lives. Our faith grows, for example, in the area of leading people to Christ, in receiving healing, in receiving the baptism of the Holy Spirit, in receiving God's provision for us in the material realm, in receiving His guidance, and so forth.

One of the first areas in which I remember seeing my own faith grow was the area of God's provision for me in the material realm. After I became a Christian and began to attend seminary, I had to learn to rely upon God to provide my needs. I read and re-read God's promises for provision, especially the sections of Scripture in Philippians 4:19 and Matthew 6:25-34. I knew *God had said* that if I would seek His kingdom and righteousness first, my material needs would be met. I knew He provided for other people by faith; yet it seemed so remote to me that He would do the same thing for me.

Though I read and re-read God's Word, I still wondered: Would God do the same for me? I knew *His Word said He would,* but somehow my faith had not grown to the point that I could rest in and act on that Word. My sleep at night was fitful and restless, and even my stomach churned. *I knew I needed more faith, so I kept confessing the Word of God.* I began to see God move people to give toward the support of my very young and small ministry. I only needed $500 a month at that time to pay all my bills; and as I began to grow in faith in that area, I entered into God's rest in the process.

Several years later, after I had finished seminary and my ministry had grown larger, I realized that the monthly budget for the ministry had grown to $15,000 a month, or $500 *a day!* Then I realized something else very wonderful! *I was resting.* Something had changed. I was resting in the rest of faith, trusting God and His Word. *My faith had actually grown faster than our budget!*

As people notice the soaring rate of inflation, I often hear them say, "We don't know what we're going to do." I can tell you what to do. Just make your faith grow at least 18-20% a year, if that is the inflation rate. You will be able to keep operating in the same rest of God as your faith grows, regardless of what happens to the monetary system. You will continually be able to praise and glorify Him, regardless of your circumstances.

I have learned from my own experience that if we have an area of *restlessness* in our own lives, our faith has to grow in that area until we enter into the rest of God in that portion of our Christian lives. **When we learn how to rest in the rest of faith, we will be more active than we ever have been before.** It is out of that rest and relaxation in Him that all of our actions and activities flow.

There is one thing I want to emphasize about our growth with God the Father and our fellowship with each other, and that is the outward focus of our vision. Not only does our faith have to grow that we might benefit from the increased faith that releases the power and blessing of God to us, but *our faith should also be growing in order that God might give increased releases of power and blessing for others through us.* **We should never cease being fruitful for the benefit of others.**

I would like to share with you how my faith grew in the area of receiving and ministering the baptism in the Holy Spirit. I was baptized in the Holy Spirit in a FGBMFI convention in Washington, D.C. Having read a *Voice* Magazine and realizing I didn't have the gift of speaking in tongues (though I wanted it), the Lord spoke to me and said, "Go to Washington to the next FGBMFI convention, and I will baptize you in the Holy Spirit there."

I did what the Lord told me. I went to Washington and was in a meeting when the invitation was given for those to come forward who wanted to be baptized in the Holy Spirit. I stayed in the back of the auditorium where I was seated because, then, I was very cautious and still a rigid Presbyterian! I carefully watched what was happening. Men and women were praying for those who wanted to be baptized in the Spirit, and I began to hear the beautiful languages coming forth from their lips. I thought, "Well, that *is* nice." Then I said to the Lord:

"You told me to come down here to receive this blessing. So I know I'm going to receive it because You told me You were going to give it to me here. But I don't want to go up there with all those people, and I certainly don't want to raise my hands the way they're raising theirs! Lord, just give me Your blessing now, right here, while I'm alone with You in the back of this auditorium."

I had obviously placed certain restrictions upon the Lord, but He was gracious enough to meet me in spite of them. While I was watching some of those people being baptized in the Holy Spirit, He spoke directly to me and said very powerfully, *Roxanne, raise your hands and praise Me!* I didn't understand that raising your hands is a way to praise God and thought it was pointless; but the Lord's words were so strong that I obeyed Him and raised my hands. I didn't know how to praise Him because I was such a baby Christian. All I knew by memory were two portions of Scripture, the Lord's Prayer and the 23rd Psalm.

I raised my hands, opened my mouth, and was about to say, "Our Father who art in heaven." (That's how little I knew about praise.) The next thing I knew, however, something like a lightning bolt hit me, and I said, *Ai yi yi.* That surge of power shocked me, and after those first seemingly uninspired syllables, another type of language began to pour out of my mouth. All kinds of beautiful sounds with certain phrases kept pouring out of my mouth, and I repeated some of the phrases again and again. God had a special surprise for me, too, for a little Jewish-Christian woman and a theologian who knew Hebrew came near me and heard me speak in Hebrew a phrase that meant, *Oh, what happiness, what joy.* I kept speaking for a long time. There was such power around me that when the little Jewish lady tried to touch me, she fell over on the floor. I had no idea of how the power of God worked, and it startled me to see it. I thought, *My, what have I done?* I didn't know the Holy Spirit did those things.

After a while the lady found she could touch me without falling back, and she began to pray for me. Then she said to me, "Roxanne, I feel that the Lord would have you come and pray for other people with me. You need to learn how to do this because He shows me that it will be very important for your ministry.''

I agreed. Then I began to follow her around as she prayed for men and women who wanted the baptism in the Holy Spirit. She would put each of her hands on someone and, two by two, the Lord Jesus would baptize them in the Holy Spirit. She motioned to me and said, "Come here and put your hands on these people, too, Roxanne." She said she wanted me to pray for them with her, so I did.

Many people were baptized in the Holy Spirit. Then we began praying for two men to be baptized. I placed one hand on each man's back, closed my eyes, and prayed in my new language. When I opened my eyes, however, the little lady had disappeared, and I couldn't see her in the crowd.

I thought, *Oh no, these men want to be baptized in the Holy Spirit, but she's gone. She has all the power, so now they won't be baptized. What should I do?*

Then I thought, *I'll just keep praying in my language while I look for her.* I didn't want to interrupt the men because they were praying so earnestly. I couldn't see her anywhere. Then I felt some of the muscles in the back of each man start to move. Their hands shot up; while one began to pray in tongues, the other started to sing in tongues. They got what they were expecting — the Holy Spirit came and filled them to overflowing.

I was thrilled and amazed. I thought, *This is wonderful! God has done this without the little lady present. If He can baptize two people with His Spirit while I pray, then He can do it many, many times again.* You couldn't stop me for the rest of the afternoon. I was putting my hands on people, praying for them, and Jesus was filling them with His Spirit!

Do you see what happened? God put me in a corner where I *had* to pray, where I *had* to move in His Word, even if I didn't want to. When I moved in response to His nudges and prayed with the faith that I had, He began to honor that faith. Even that day, the seed of faith began to grow and sprout. **My seed of faith to minister the baptism of the Holy Spirit grew, not only a few inches, but maybe even a foot that day!**

On my way home to Boston the next day, the Lord spoke to me and said, *You're going to have a difficult time trying to explain what has happened to you to those who don't know Me, Roxanne. But there are many people who need to receive Me as their Savior and to be baptized in the Holy Spirit as well.*

The Lord opened up all kinds of places for me to speak — in chapels, in small groups, and at the hospital where I visited the sick. I went back to my old prep school, *Dana Hall,* in Wellesley, Massachusetts, and was invited to speak in the morning chapel hour. After I spoke and told them about Jesus dying for our sins, being resurrected and living for us, some of the people asked if I could come again and speak to them more personally in small groups, which I did.

Many of these women I spoke to were quite fashionable; and although they received the truth of Jesus as Savior and Lord, I didn't see just how they would even want to receive the baptism of the Holy Spirit. The Lord was so good, however; He showed me just how to present His truth. I did as He told me, and all those ladies received the baptism in the Holy Spirit. In fact, ten of them were filled with the Spirit in one evening at a small meeting.

I realized that the Lord could baptize more than two people in His Spirit at one time. Later, while I was in seminary, I saw the Lord baptize even more people at one time. I went to a retreat with a beautiful man named David DuPlessis, who showed me how to minister the baptism in the Holy Spirit another way. He told me Jesus could baptize any number of people in the Holy Spirit at once if they wanted Him to. At that retreat, when we prayed, about 100 people were baptized in the Spirit at the same time.

What was changing? What was growing? My faith was growing. In the course of approximately six months, I saw Jesus baptize first 2 people, then 10 people, then 100 people. I thought, *If Jesus can do this, He can baptize hundreds or even thousands of Christians at the same time.*

A number of months later, I was speaking in a Methodist church to approximately 300 people. The pastor told me that about half of the people were filled with the Spirit. That evening, as I spoke on Jesus the Baptizer and the baptism in the Holy Spirit, I felt a sense of the presence of Jesus fill the sanctuary.

Toward the end of the service, my eyes were opened and I saw Jesus standing at the back of the auditorium. He didn't walk, but somehow He moved up the aisle. When He reached the front, He turned toward the people. It was so still you could have heard a pin drop. His presence was so real and so powerful! Then He raised His hands; and immediately, I heard a low murmur of tongues begin to flow all through that sanctuary. It sounded like a river of tongues as it rose in volume. Later, the pastor of the church told me that 150 people were baptized in the Holy Spirit that night.

When I look back at these experiences and see what God did, I realize that He did it through my faith. Our faith can release God to work or it can limit His ability to work. In the beginning, I had a tiny seed of faith; and it hadn't grown much in the area of ministering the baptism of the Holy Spirit. When Jesus answered my prayer and filled two people with His Spirit, that seed sprouted. When He filled ten people as I prayed, my faith grew some more. When 100 people were filled, my faith grew from *little* faith to *more* faith. Then, when 150 people were filled that night, my faith in that area grew to *great* faith.

I know very well that Jesus could baptize thousands of people in the Holy Spirit at one time if the meeting were large enough. I want to say, however, that while I have great faith to minister the baptism in the Holy Spirit, I don't have great faith in every area of my life just yet. Where I have less faith, however, I try to feed and nurture it to make it grow.

As Christians, we are all alike in that our faith is greater in some areas than in others. We have different levels or amounts of faith for different things, but **we should consciously work to make our faith grow in all areas of our lives by hearing and acting on God's Word.**

Because some people haven't understood this truth, they have had their faith damaged by trying to act on faith that wasn't sufficiently developed to do what they were asking God to do through them. If that has happened to you, you shouldn't be discouraged, rather you should go back to work in that area. Others who have seen this area of truth have used it to their advantage. Let's look at that next.

3

From Weak to Strong

Different Levels of Faith

The Bible says that Abraham wasn't **weak** in faith, but he was **strong** in faith (Rom. 4:19, 20). This shows us that there are indeed **different strengths, amounts,** or **levels** of faith. It is the same kind of faith God talks about throughout His Word, but there are different levels of that same faith.

We already mentioned how Jesus spoke of *no* faith (Mark 4:40), of *little* faith (Matt. 14:31), and of *great* faith (Matt. 8:10; 15:28). These different levels of faith accomplish different jobs in God's kingdom, just as different strengths or amounts of power are needed to do different jobs in the natural realm.

Recently, for example, we had to have some land cleared surrounding our Christian Center in Northern Florida. The contractor we worked with explained what he would use for the different jobs we needed to have done. To push out small pine trees, he said we would need a small D-3 bulldozer. To push out large oaks, we would need a medium-sized D-6, which is larger. To remove a hill and fill a sinkhole, a large D-10 bulldozer was needed. The respective amounts of power these three machines put forth were 36,000, 55,000, and 270,000 pounds of drawbar pull or push. Obviously, a little bulldozer could move a small tree, but it couldn't move a "mountain." You can see that just as we require different strengths or amounts of force to accomplish different-sized jobs in the natural realm, so also we require different *strengths, levels,* or *amounts* of faith to accomplish different-sized jobs in God's kingdom.

Too Little Faith

This important truth — that different strengths or levels of faith are needed to accomplish different-sized jobs in God's kingdom — was clearly illustrated by Jesus' teaching in the following passage of Scripture:

And when they were come to the multitude, there came to him a certain man, kneeling down to him, and saying,

Lord, have mercy on my son: for he is lunatic, and sore vexed: for ofttimes he falleth into the fire, and oft into the water.

And I brought him to thy disciples, and they could not cure him.

Then Jesus answered and said, O faithless and perverse generation, how long shall I be with you? how long shall I suffer you? bring him hither to me.

And Jesus rebuked the devil; and he departed out of him: and the child was cured from that very hour.

Then came the disciples to Jesus apart, and said, Why could not we cast him out?

And Jesus said unto them, Because of your unbelief: for verily I say unto you, If ye have faith as a grain of mustard seed, ye shall say unto this mountain, Remove hence to yonder place; and it shall remove; and nothing shall be impossible unto you.

Howbeit this kind goeth not out but by prayer and fasting (Matt. 17:14-21).

Jesus had just come down from the Mountain of Transfiguration where He had been filled with the effulgence of the glory of God, and He had experienced what we have come to know as the Transfiguration. His face had shone as the sun, and His clothing had been white as the light.

When He came down into the valley, however, He was met by the father we just read about. The father brought a bad progress report to the Master concerning His disciples. What he said, in essence, was, "Lord, your disciples don't have what it takes to set my son free. They can't deliver the goods, so have mercy and help me." Jesus, in turn, asked the disciples how long He was going to have to put up with their powerlessness, their lack of faith.

When the disciples saw their failure and Jesus' success, they asked Him why they couldn't do the job. In the King James Version of the Bible, Jesus appears to say they didn't have any faith, but rather had unbelief. That is incorrect. The Greek word *oligopistian* (from the Greek words: *oligos* meaning "little" or "small," and *pistis* meaning "faith") is not accurately translated here. It should be translated *little faith.*

Jesus said to the disciples, *Because of your little faith, you could not cast the demon out of the young boy*. Other Bible scholars have translated this as follows:

"Because you have so little faith." (*NIV* and *Phillips*)

"Because your faith is too weak." (*NEB*)

"Because of the littleness of your faith." (*Amplified* and *NASB*).

*The problem was they did not have **enough** faith to do the job*. That is what Jesus told them. Unbelief is a strong negative force. Even reason tells us that someone with *unbelief* doesn't even believe in demons, much less have the power to cast them out of a person. Obviously, the disciples had some faith because they tried to cast the demon out of the boy. *They just didn't have enough faith to be effective*. **Likewise, the reason for so much of our ineffectiveness today is a lack of sufficient faith.**

Jesus didn't just scold the disciples for not having enough faith. When they asked Him, He told them how to get more faith. He said, "Let your faith grow like a mustard seed. Then, when it's fully matured, not only can you move a mountain with your faith, but *nothing* will be impossible for you."

Even though the disciples had little faith at that time, Jesus assured them that with time and with proper feeding and exercise, faith could become a tremendous force for them.

It is very easy for me to understand why Christians living in North America have so little faith, compared with the Christians who live in South America. In the United States, it is very easy for us to hear the Good News of Jesus Christ and to receive Him. However, even after we are filled with the Holy Spirit, we rarely depend on Him as Christians in poorer countries must. If we have a headache, we can always get an aspirin. If we are hungry, we can reach into our pocket for money. If a light bulb goes out, we can go to the store and buy a new one.

The Christians in South America, however, have to go to God and depend upon Him for everything. If they don't have enough milk for their children, they must ask the Lord to do something. When the only light bulb over the pulpit in a little mountain church goes out, they can't run to the store. They simply pray over the old one and ask the Lord to make it work — and He does, because they expect Him to. When they are hungry, they have to depend upon the Lord for the next meal — and He moves on someone to share with them.

They use their faith muscles all the time. God answers their prayers, and their faith grows continually. That is why their faith level is higher than the faith level of the average Spirit-filled Christian in North America.

*In summary, Jesus wants us to learn from this account of the disciples and the demon-possessed boy that **there are different levels of faith needed to perform different jobs in His kingdom**.* Therefore, our faith can grow and become more effective, just as the mustard seed can grow from a very small seed to a large plant.

Four, Eight, and Twelve Feet of Faith

I often talk about *four, eight, and twelve feet of faith* referring to *little faith, medium-sized faith,* and *great faith,* respectively. When people ask me about my use of those figures, I explain that a mustard tree grows to twelve feet in height and there are three basic levels of faith.

The smallest amount of faith, or *little faith,* would be anything from a sprout to four feet. Similarly, faith that grows from four to eight feet in height would be *medium-sized faith,* and that which grows from eight to twelve feet would be *great* or *mountain-moving faith.* Then, there are situations where more than great faith is required. For example, if you need 25 feet or more of faith for a miracle, that is when you need the supernatural *gift of faith* from God which is listed in 1 Corinthians 12.

If you have *little faith* — anything I call *up to four feet of faith* — *you have plenty of faith for a sinus healing, an earache healing, or a healing for arthritis in your hands.* However, you have *too little faith for healing blindness, deafness, or terminal cancer.* This truth is important for you to grasp. **You need to know if your faith needs more time to grow before you can receive a healing or pray for someone else to be healed of blindness, deafness, or terminal cancer.**

Some people can actually tempt God without knowing it. They pray to Him and ask Him to do something without giving Him enough of their faith with which to work. For example, let's say you are a potter. I come to you with a golf-ball-size piece of clay and ask you to make me a beautiful vase to hold flowers. You say, "Roxanne, it takes 50 times more clay to make the pot you want than what you have brought me." You would be justified in telling me that I have asked the impossible. It wouldn't be your fault if I turned away disappointed.

Many times when we ask God to do something big for us, He looks down and says, "You haven't given Me enough faith with which to do the job."

For example, if you have an appendicitis attack at 3:00 a.m. and feel your appendix rupture, you know in the natural realm that in a short period of time you will die. **What will you do?**

If you have *little* faith, if you are *weak* in faith, you can ask God to heal you right then, but the answer you will hear is, *I can't heal you by your faith. You don't have enough faith for Me to work with.* It would be much better for you to pray, go to a hospital, and believe God to work through more natural means until your faith has grown to the place where you can receive that tremendous miracle. (That is what Smith Wigglesworth did when his appendix ruptured.)

It is important to realize that you need *great faith* for God to move in a *great way* for you. We know God can sovereignly move by His grace and do powerful things; but if you are depending on *your* faith, you need to know whether you have enough to give Him to get the job done.

You absolutely must come to understand one fact: **Faith is a substance as real to God as clay is to you. He works with that substance.** Faith is a spiritual reality to

Him. *A lack of faith, or too little faith, can limit God or keep Him from doing the things in our lives He wishes to do or that we ask Him to do.* It is very important that you make your faith grow to the *strong or great faith levels* where He is free to work as both **He** and **you** want Him to, both for you and for others.

Faith Won't *Cop Out*

Another truth suggested in the story of Jesus' ministry, both to the demon-possessed boy and to His disciples, is that *even though our faith may not be great enough in certain situations, we can't cop out in tough places in life.*

While I believe it is definitely wrong to ask God to work miracles in our lives when we can't really believe for them, I also believe that He gives us the alternative of living a prayerful life and being guided by His Spirit in the way we are ready to walk. When we are confronted with crises, however, we have to use what faith we have, even though it may appear to our natural man that it isn't big enough.

Jesus has taught me through experience that when only a tremendous miracle can solve a difficult situation, He wants me to use my faith; and if it is needed, He will supply the gift of faith for that situation to get the job done. He has taught me that I simply cannot *cop out* in a desperate situation just because I don't have great faith.

I learned this lesson for the first time several years ago when I was ministering in the South. During a week-day communion service for ladies, a woman I casually knew began sobbing bitterly. Gently, I walked over to her and said, "Honey, what's wrong? What's bothering you so deeply?"

The woman said, "Oh, Roxanne, you just wouldn't believe how horrible it is. My sister is in the hospital with terminal cancer. She's married to a doctor who specializes in cancer surgery, and she has already lived two weeks past the date they said she would die. I called her this morning, as I do every morning and evening to see how she is, to see if she's still alive. She's nothing but bones. She's lost all her hair, and the stench is horrible. I know that is bad enough, but it is so hard for me to telephone. I have to brace myself because I never know if the nurses are going to tell me she's already dead."

She continued to sob, and I did the only reasonable thing I could do: I prayed.

I put my hand on the sobbing woman and began to pray, "Dear Jesus, walk into her sister's room. Go into that hospital room and put Your arms around that cancer-ridden, bony body. Jesus, let the resurrection power of Your Spirit burn the cancer out of that body and work a creative miracle. Heal, restore, and raise up that woman."

As I was finishing my prayer, the power of God suddenly hit me like a bolt of lightning. I stood there, shaking, my knees almost buckling. What power! I felt this tremendous power surge through me! And more than that, **I knew with every cell of my being that the woman in the hospital was healed!** I felt as if I had been given *100 feet of faith!* I knew God had given me *the gift of faith,* but I also knew it hadn't come to anyone else around me just then. The people around me knew

God *could* heal anyone, but that's not faith. I knew He *had* healed that woman. *That is faith!*

I turned to the woman who had been sobbing and said, "Friend, your sister has just been healed! The Lord has just done it."

She said to me, "But, Roxanne, what if she's dead? I haven't called since 7:00 this morning, and she might have died already."

I told her, "Honey, even if your sister had died since you called, I have felt so much faith that I know she's resurrected now!" I went back to my seat and sat down. I knew that woman was healed!

In a case like this, I believe the gift of faith extends over a period of time; it concentrates on results and on goals, not on the process needed to get there. Consequently, it was about three months later that I received a letter from that lady. She began her letter, "Dear Roxanne, *you won't believe this!*" I just laughed when I read that since *she* was the one who had the trouble believing it!

She went on, "My sister was the lady you prayed for three months ago, and now the cancer has completely left her body. She has a full head of hair and is running around, jogging with her husband. She is in better health now than she's been in for most of her life. Jesus has completely and perfectly healed her, and everyone is giving thanks to God."

The Lord taught me through that situation that even though I had little faith or just medium-sized faith for healing at that time in my ministry, when a desperate situation presented itself, I should pray or sometimes fast and pray; and God would give me the gift of faith when necessary to do the job effectively.

When Jesus told His disciples, concerning the demon-possessed boy, that those kind didn't go out except by prayer and fasting, He was teaching that prayer and fasting can *aid* our faith in difficult situations. *When we pray and fast, we are putting the outer man in subjection to the inner man;* we are dealing with increasing our capacity for faith by giving attention to the things of God through prayer, fasting, and meditation on the Word. We shouldn't think there is any other way to *gain faith* than by hearing the Word of God.

Another truth about faith levels came as a surprise when Jesus first revealed it to me. Although I understood that there are different levels of faith — what I have referred to as four, eight, and twelve feet of faith — I didn't understand that **we can have different levels of faith in different areas of our lives.** For example, you may have *four feet of faith for God's finances for you, eight feet of faith for healing,* and *seven feet to minister the baptism in the Holy Spirit.*The fact that we often have different levels of faith in different areas of our lives is an important principle which I did not understand until Jesus spoke to me several years ago about some business I was trying to accomplish for Him.

Different Levels of Faith In Different Areas

A number of years ago, when our organization was growing quickly, I was aware that we needed an accountant. I asked the Lord to show me how to get a good Christian accountant or bookkeeper. After I prayed, I didn't feel any specific direction, so I did the most practical thing I could: I notified the local employment bureau and ran an ad in the newspaper.

After about a week, we hadn't received any response, so I prayed again. I said, "Lord, You know we need a bookkeeper, and I know You are the Head of this ministry. It's Your ministry, not mine, so what are You going to do about providing a bookkeeper for us?"

The Lord answered me in words that left warm, clear impressions in my spirit. He said, "Roxanne, take the ad out of the paper. Withdraw the application from the employment bureau. I have already chosen the man for the job, and he will come into your office the day after tomorrow" (which he did).

Then He continued: "The man I have chosen hasn't seen the ad. I have sovereignly spoken to him, and he will come to you." I was amazed when I heard that. Then, as the Lord continued speaking, I learned something new: "Roxanne, you have *much* faith for healing, *much* faith to minister the baptism in the Holy Spirit, *much* faith that I can speak through you whatever I want. *But you have very little faith that I can speak sovereignly to someone else and bring that person to you.*"

I was shocked, but I knew it was true! *Jesus was showing me that my levels of faith were very different in those different areas.* I saw, of course, that the same thing must be true for all of us. As the Lord said, the man arrived on the appointed day and became our bookkeeper. He had overheard a conversation between some Christians who knew about our need; and the Spirit of the Lord came over him and said, "Sam, you are the man for that job." He had just taken an early retirement and had been a bookkeeper all his life. The Lord told him there was still more for him to do in His service.

If we have different levels of faith in various areas of our lives, what determines the difference? The answer is quite simple. **We will have more faith in the areas where we have read, heard, confessed, and acted on the Word of God.** Someone who reads Psalm 91 every day will have more faith for God's protection than a Christian who has only read that Psalm perhaps ten times.

The same laws of growth are evident everywhere in the natural realm, so why should you be surprised if they apply in the supernatural as well?

For example, if a weightlifter wants to grow stronger, he doesn't immediately go to his goal of 500 pounds. He begins to exercise his muscles on small amounts of iron. He may even begin with a few pounds in each hand and the determination to exercise faithfully. As he is consistent, his muscles respond; he then picks up larger weights in each hand — 25, 50, and eventually even 100 pounds in each hand. As he consistently works, keeping his mind on his goal, he doesn't become discouraged; but, rather, his confidence grows with each new step of strength. When he has reached his goal of being able to lift 500 pounds, he knows his strength and sees the fruit of all his diligent application.

So it is with the growth of faith. We don't begin by tackling things too large for us. We begin with several scriptures, promising something we need, and believe God's Word the best we can. We begin confessing and acting on His Word, meditating on it, and watching our faith grow. With our eyes on the goal of *great* faith, we move from *little* faith to *medium-sized,* or *strong,* faith.

Daily and consistently, we see growth and are encouraged. We not only keep looking forward to the goal of great faith, but we also look back to the various steps we have made in faith and the knowledge of God's Word. The facts about the growth of faith and levels of faith should encourage us to operate within the laws of God regarding faith, instead of becoming discouraged by our ignorance of them.

Be aware of the stages in your faith growth. Know when you have moved from *little* faith to *medium-sized* faith to *great* faith in each area of your life. Above all, *keep using your faith continually*. Don't stop exercising it just because you had a great faith victory. **Keep on!** *What limit can you put on God?*

David came before Saul and said, *Thy servant will go and fight this Philistine.* Saul judged David by what he saw and responded, *Thou art not able to go against this Philistine to fight with him: for thou art but a youth, and he a man of war from his youth* (1 Sam. 17:32, 33).

But David answered Saul and declared that he had already tested and proven his faith.

Thy servant kept his father's sheep, and there came a lion, and a bear, and took a lamb out of the flock:

And I went out after him, and smote him, and delivered it out of his mouth: and when he arose against me, I caught him by his beard, and smote him, and slew him.

Thy servant slew both the lion and the bear: and this uncircumcised Philistine shall be as one of them, seeing he hath defied the armies of the living God.

David said moreover, The Lord that delivered me out of the paw of the lion, and out of the paw of the bear, he will deliver me out of the hand of this Philistine. And Saul said unto David, Go, and the Lord be with thee (1 Sam. 17:34-37).

This passage reveals David's growth of faith in God's covenant Word through successive tests. No doubt, he knew the promises of Deuteronomy 28 among all the other promises for deliverance and protection; and he exercised his faith by putting it to work. As He saw God's delivering power, his faith grew. Later, *when he needed great faith,* his faith was great, ready and strong, *because it had been tested, tried, and increased* in his battles with the lion and bear. David was ready to believe. He *knew* that God would give him victory over Goliath.

Just as you have to pass the tests of elementary school and high school before going to college, so you have to pass the tests of little and medium-sized faith before entering the level of great faith that is required for great miracles. We all grow through these stages, but *some will grow faster because they have set their eyes on a goal and have applied themselves to the exercises of faith with faithfulness and diligence.*

We have learned that faith does grow and that there are levels of faith through which we grow. Now let's look more closely at the process of increasing our faith.

4

How to Increase *Your* Faith

Most Christians know that *faith cometh by hearing, and hearing by the word of God* (Rom. 10:17). If faith comes by hearing the Word of God, then it follows that **faith will increase the more we hear the Word.** When God says that faith comes by hearing His Word, He means hearing in such a way that we **believe, confess,** and **act on that Word.**

For example, God has said, *Hear, and your soul shall live* (Is. 55:3). God means that we have to **hear** Him, not just with our outer ears, but with the ears of our spirits — **hear** Him in such a way that we **believe** and **act** on His Word.

Yes, faith comes and grows by hearing the Word of God — by believing, confessing, and acting on the Word in our everyday lives. However, I do not believe we can appreciate how closely connected the reception and growth of faith is with the Word of God until we see and understand the tremendous **creative power** in the Word.

GOD'S WORD IS CREATIVE. IT'S ALIVE!

God's Word has the power to:

create faith
So then faith cometh by hearing, and hearing by the word of God (Rom. 10:17).

bring about the new birth

Being born again, not of corruptible seed, but of incorruptible, by the word of God, which liveth and abideth for ever (1 Pet. 1:23).

heal and deliver

He sent his word, and healed them, and delivered them from their destructions (Ps. 107:20).

cleanse

Now ye are clean through the word which I have spoken unto you (John 15:3).

create the universe

By the word of the Lord were the heavens made; and all the host of them by the breath of his mouth (Ps. 33:6).

nourish and produce fruit

For as the rain cometh down, and the snow from heaven, and returneth not thither, but watereth the earth, and maketh it bring forth and bud, that it may give seed to the sower, and bread to the eater: So shall my word be that goeth forth out of my mouth: it shall not return unto me void, but it shall accomplish that which I please, and it shall prosper in the thing whereto I sent it (Is. 55:10, 11).

give life and strength

This is my comfort in my affliction: for thy word hath quickened me (Ps. 119:50).

give understanding

The entrance of thy words giveth light; it giveth understanding unto the simple (Ps. 119:130).

It can do much, much more for you!

There is tremendous creative power in God's Word. It is important that you see this. **The whole natural realm is subject to the Spirit-anointed Word of God through which it was created.** We see this again and again in the Scriptures. Joshua, in his battle against the kings of the Amorites, needed more light to fight them. He spoke in the power of the Spirit, before all Israel, saying:

> *Sun, stand thou still upon Gibeon; and thou, Moon, in the valley of Ajalon.*
>
> *And the sun stood still, and the moon stayed, until the people had avenged themselves upon their enemies* (Joshua 10:12, 13).

Look at the power of that creative, Spirit-anointed Word of God! If the sun and moon stopped, that means the earth's rotation was suspended. The natural laws were subject to the authority of that Spirit-empowered Word.

The natural realm was created out of the supernatural realm and is, therefore, subject to the supernatural. Until we see that revelation, we will never fully understand the tremendous power in the Word of God. **The Word of God that created the universe still dominates it today.** The whole natural realm was brought into being by the creative Word of God.

When God said, "Universe, vegetable kingdom, animal kingdom, come into being!" the whole natural realm was manifested through the instrumentality of the Spirit-empowered Word of God. The Bible declares that the worlds were framed by the Word of God and things which are seen were not made of things which appear (Heb. 11:3). As a consequence, *the creative Source remains of greater power than the creation, and the Word of God still dominates the natural creation.*

Look at the examples in Scripture when this was evident. In Mark 11:12-14, Jesus approached a fig tree expecting to find fruit on it. When He didn't find fruit, He said, *No man eat fruit of thee hereafter for ever. And His disciples heard it* (Mark 11:14). When they returned from Jerusalem, they passed the same tree and found it dried from the roots. Peter was amazed and said to Jesus: *Master, behold, the fig tree which thou cursedst is withered away* (Mark 11:21).

Jesus answered him with an exhortation: *Have faith in God* (Mark 11:22). A better translation is, "Have the faith **of** God." Then Jesus spoke what has become the most celebrated faith scripture in the Bible:

> *For verily I say unto you, That whosoever shall say unto this mountain, Be thou removed, and be thou cast into the sea; and shall not doubt in his heart, but shall believe that those things which he saith shall come to pass; he shall have whatsoever he saith* (Mark 11:23).

Jesus was saying to Peter, "Peter, I want you to understand that **the natural realm is subject to the spiritual realm.** When you release the faith of God in your heart and speak faith — the Word of faith — to something in the natural realm, **those faith-filled words release God's power all around you. Then the natural realm has to submit to the supernatural.**"

That is what happened to the fig tree; that is why it dried up. It had no choice! It couldn't do anything else because **the natural realm has to submit. This is God's order.**

Another time, we see Jesus, the Living Word of God, asleep in a ship on the Sea of Galilee when a tremendous storm arose. The ship was in danger of sinking, so the disciples awoke Jesus. They cried out to Him, *Master, carest thou not that we perish? And He arose, and rebuked the wind, and said unto the sea, Peace, be still. And the wind ceased, and there was a great calm* (Mark 4:38, 39). Here we see the Living Word rise up and speak a Word that stilled a storm. **We see the Word of God still dominating the universe. We see the natural order yielding to the Word of God.**

That same creative Word was spoken to ten lepers who needed to be healed. They had already seen or heard of Jesus' ministry; and when He entered a village where they were standing afar off watching Him, they cried out: "Jesus, heal us!" He simply said to them, *Go shew yourselves unto the priests. And it came to pass, that, as they went, they were cleansed* (Luke 17:14). Those bodies had to come into line with the Word of God because they were products of the natural realm.

Another place in Scripture where we see the creative, spoken Word of God is in the account of *the resurrection of Lazarus.* By the time Jesus arrived at Bethany, Lazarus had been dead four days; and Martha didn't want Jesus to have the stone rolled away because his body would already be stinking. Jesus knew the power of the supernatural was greater than the natural forces of decomposition, so He asked Martha, *Said I not unto thee, that, if thou wouldest believe, thou shouldest see the glory of God?* (John 11:40). Then Jesus *cried with a loud voice, Lazarus, come forth* (John 11:43). The next verse says, *And he that was dead came forth bound hand and foot with graveclothes: and his face was bound about with a napkin.*

The people were stupefied! They were amazed! **They had seen the creative Word of God go down into a piece of rotten human flesh and recreate what death had already begun to destroy.**

That Word had exploded throughout Lazarus' body. It shut off the decomposing processes within his body, turned them around, and began to loose its creative power everywhere.

In the midst of all that stench, the Word went to work and life began to pour into that body. Healing power began to flood into every cell.

Then Lazarus' spirit and soul came back into his body. He stood up and walked out of the darkness of that tomb into the sunshine and light of day.

Jesus never touched him; He never had to touch him. **All the power needed for that tremendous miracle was resident in the creative Word of God.** Jesus believed in His heart and spoke God's creative Word with His mouth and the natural order came into conformity with what Jesus had believed and spoken.

What power there is in that creative Word of God! The universe can't stop it! If we will that it works in our lives and don't stop it by doubting or unbelief, then we will see God's power released. When our lives are in

line with God's Word as we speak and act on that
Word, that same supernatural power will bring things
into visible manifestation before us.

The Word Transforms Gideon and YOU!

*The power of God's creative Word to transform a
human life is clearly illustrated in the life of Gideon,*
recorded in Judges 6. When the Word of God first came
to Gideon, he was living under the oppression of the
occupying Midianite army. He was threshing wheat by
a winepress, instead of on a regular threshing floor, so
his harvest wouldn't be confiscated by the enemy.

*Gideon was afraid; he was hiding from his
enemies;* and at that time, the angel of the Lord
appeared to him and said, *The Lord is with thee, thou
mighty man of valour* (Judges 6:12). God's faith was
obviously being spoken because, as yet, there was
nothing mighty or valorous in Gideon's life.

Gideon's theology was wrong. He thought the day
of miracles was past (v. 13). Also, *his response was
wrong* because he looked to himself instead of to God
and God's power to accomplish the job (v. 14).

However, the Word of God kept coming to
Gideon, **working in him** — assuring him, directing him,
transforming him, bringing him increased faith and
power. As he **heard** that Word and **responded to it,**
Gideon finally **became** what the Word of the Lord
(spoken at first by the angel) said he already was — **a
mighty man of valor!**

This is a principle that God has applied, not only
to Gideon, but also to us. **If the Word of God can**

change a man like Gideon, it can change you and me.
We must simply expose ourselves to the Word and get it
working in our hearts. If the Word is able to make the
sun and moon stand still, quiet a raging storm,
resurrect a dead man's body, wither a tree, and cleanse
leprosy, then it is certainly more than powerful enough
to change you and me! Hebrews 4:12 states that God's
Word is full of His power and life:

> *For the word of God is quick, and powerful,
> and sharper than any twoedged sword, piercing
> even to the dividing asunder of soul and spirit, and
> of the joints and marrow, and is a discerner of the
> thoughts and intents of the heart.*

When you begin to be absorbed in God's Word,
really hearing it in your heart so that you believe it,
then that Living Word can begin its work in you. The
Bible assures us that **the Word does work in us when we
believe it, speak it, and act on it.** Paul made that
declaration to the Thessalonian Christians, knowing it
to be true from his own experience:

> *For this cause also thank we God without
> ceasing, because, when ye received the word of
> God which ye heard of us, ye received it not as the
> word of men, but as it is in truth, the word of
> God, which effectually worketh also in you that
> believe* (1 Thess. 2:13).

He was telling the Thessalonians that the Word of
God was an effective and powerful force in their lives
which continued to perform its work in them as they
continued to believe. He became excited about the way
they received it and believed it because he knew what it

would do in their lives. He knew what it had done to Gideon and to a man named Saul, who had once set out for Damascus to persecute Christians.

We have repeatedly stressed that faith comes by hearing God's creative Word, and we can see further examples of that truth:

The woman with the issue of blood for twelve years received her healing because she **heard** about Jesus and kept **saying** she would be healed if she could only touch His coat. (Mark 5:25-34.)

How did Cornelius and all his household receive faith for salvation? By the words which Peter preached. He **heard** those words and **believed** them. (Acts 11: 4-18.)

Faith for anything God has provided comes by hearing His Word.

Many Christians know that faith **comes** by hearing (which includes reading, meditating on, and confessing) God's Words. They also know that faith **grows** by hearing God's Word and by acting on it. Though many Christians know this, most of them underestimate the importance of speaking aloud or confessing the Word of God. They do not understand the tremendous power resident in God's spoken Words to accomplish many things. The Bible teaches that *what you say* (over a period of time) *is what you get;* or what you confess with a believing heart you will, in time, possess in your life.

Confession Brings Possession

The truth that *confession brings possession* is seen throughout God's Word. The consistent believing and confessing of God's Word on a daily basis increases your faith and brings into manifestation those promises of God that you have confessed.

There is one point I want to emphasize here: It is the **consistent daily confession** of God's promises, the holding fast to His Word and agreeing with Him over a period of time, that brings His promises into manifestation in our lives.

The writer of Hebrews exhorts us to *hold fast to our profession* because we have a great High Priest, Jesus Christ, who has taken His place in heaven as the High Priest of our profession. In Hebrews 4:14 and 3:1, the word *profession* is a translation of the Greek word we normally translate "confession." It means "to say the same thing as" or "to agree with." **We are to agree with what God says about us in His Word and agree with what He says His Word will do.**

We are to hold onto our confession, even in the face of apparent defeat or failure. We are to speak forth the Word of God and act on that Word until the evidence of our senses lines up with the Word. Once that Word was the Word on God's lips, then it was the Word on the lips of Joshua, Isaiah, Jesus, Paul, and Peter. Now it is the Word of God on **your** lips that will release God's power. **You are your own faith-builder as you speak forth the Word of the Lord.**

As you speak forth God's Word, your faith increases; and that continual believing and confessing of God's Word builds up the level of your faith until your faith releases the power of God around you to meet the need you have in your life. Truly, God hastens to fulfill His Word. He watches over His Word to perform it, just as He said in Jeremiah 1:12, **His Word is meant to be used by the heirs of salvation.**

We need to identify with God in the way He works. You see, God is a **speaking** God, and He is a **faith** God. In the very beginning, at Creation, God believed and spoke out of a heart full of faith. Later He saw the results of His speaking. They were magnificent results. We are created in His likeness and in His image; and since God's actions reveal His spiritual laws of speaking action-producing results, He tells us that **we must watch the words of our mouths.**

The Apostle James wrote that, although small, the tongue is very powerful, like the rudder of a ship or the bit in a horse's mouth. Although James says man can't tame his own tongue, **it is the power that can direct our lives if we bring it under God's control. Only God can control the tongue!** James writes:

> *Behold, we put bits in the horses' mouths, that they may obey us; and we turn about their whole body.*
>
> *Behold also the ships, which though they be so great, and are driven of fierce winds, yet are they turned about with a very small helm, whithersoever the governor listeth.*
>
> *Even so the tongue is a little member, and boasteth great things. Behold, how great a matter a little fire kindleth!*

And the tongue is a fire, a world of iniquity: so is the tongue among our members, that it defileth the whole body, and setteth on fire the course of nature; and it is set on fire of hell (James 3:3-6).

While the rudder of a ship can steer it properly, it can also be the instrument of destruction if it is pointed in the wrong direction in a storm or if it guides the ship off course in dangerous water. Our tongues can run the ship of our lives onto destruction just as easily if we don't point them in the right direction. Since only God can tame the tongue (James 3:8), we need to submit our tongues to Him.

We need to put God's Word in our mouths, letting Him be Captain of the ship of our lives, knowing that our tongues can turn our lives away from the shoals that could destroy us. God's Word in our mouths can also keep our faces pointed into the wind in fierce storms. Like a ship at sea, as long as we face the storm with God's Word on our tongues, we won't be capsized. We will go through those stormy seas just as surely as God's Word is true; and we will find ourselves in peace-filled, blessing-filled waters.

Our tongues are the most powerful members in our bodies, whether for good or for evil. They will control our destinies here.

The writer of Proverbs agrees with James, for he says:

A man's belly shall be satisfied with the fruit of his mouth; and with the increase of his lips shall he be filled.

*Death and life are in the power of the tongue:
and they that love it shall eat the fruit thereof*
(Proverbs 18:20, 21).

God could not say more plainly that we will receive
what we speak into our lives. **What we confess
continually will come to us.** If we confess God's Words
of life and truth, we will eat that fruit and see the
manifestations of His life, blessing, and truth in our
lives. But just as surely, if we believe and confess the
words of fear, death, and poverty, we will see the
manifestations of fear, death, and poverty in our lives.

*Not only is the power of life and death in your
tongue, but also the power to* **change** *your life is in your
tongue.* Above everything else, you need to learn to **rest**
in the integrity of God's Word. If you really believe
what He says, you will have the assurance and peace
that the answer has *already* been received, even before
you see any outward results.

You see, learning to believe and confess God's
Word is the process Abraham learned when He
discovered how to call into being things that he couldn't
see. There is a caution to all of our faith confessions,
however: Our motives must be right. If you are one of
those Christians who is believing and confessing for two
Cadillacs, a million-dollar home, and everything in the
department store, you need to check up on the motives
of your heart. Could there possibly be some greed
between you and the promises of God?

God can do immeasurably beyond what we can
think, but we have to follow the rule Jesus decreed in
Matthew 6:33. *Put His kingdom and righteousness first
in our lives.*

Remember, Psalm 37:4 tells us that delighting ourselves completely in God will lead to His giving us the desires of our hearts. *Pure hearts bring pure results.* On the other hand, we should not fail to think large enough for God simply because some people we see confessing God's Word appear to miss the mark. God is true, even if all men are untrue (Rom. 3:3, 4); He cannot deny His Word (2 Tim. 2:13).

So be like Him. Call what you need into being by His faith; God does. He does so because He sees by faith.

In Romans 4:17, God gave us insight into both His faith and Abraham's faith. It is the Word we have just spoken about.

> *(As it is written, I have made thee a father of many nations,) before him whom he believed, even God, who quickeneth the dead, and calleth those things which be not as though they were.*

We have seen that you do, in fact, receive God's faith when you become a child of God by faith in Jesus Christ (Gal. 2:20). Now you need to use and increase that faith. If you find a promise of God that can cover a need in your life, you must begin confessing that promise in a consistent way. Then God will create the fruit of your lips, just as He said He would. (Is. 57:19.)

God gives us what we speak when we speak His Word with faith in our hearts. **Speak His Word, and you will receive His blessing.** However, if you won't correct your tongue — if you continue speaking words of unbelief, fear, and rebellion — you will receive that fruit just as certainly.

If you examine the Bible in this light, you will see it: That is exactly what happened time and again in the lives of Bible characters. For example, when the Israelites were walking in the wilderness, they grumbled and complained continuously. They didn't like God's menu of manna and quail. They kept saying, *Would God that we had died in the land of Egypt! or would God we had died in this wilderness!* (Num. 14:2). **God gave them the fruit of their lips. He granted their words.** Not one of those who murmured entered the Promised Land. Their bones were bleached in the wilderness, and God said to them before they died:

As truly as I live, saith the Lord, as ye have spoken in mine ears, so will I do to you:

Your carcases shall fall in this wilderness (Num. 14:28, 29).

And so it was; *it is a law.*

We build our faith by hearing God's Word, by feeding on it, and by confessing what God has done for us. Jesus showed me this very simply one night just before I spoke to a church congregation about how to build up their faith. The way the Holy Spirit — that blessed Spirit of Truth — showed me this surprised me. He used something I had seen on television when I was very young to illustrate the principle He wanted me to teach.

As I sat on the platform, Jesus made pictures of an old cowboy-and-Indian movie pass through my mind. There was an old steam engine being chased by Indians across a desert in the West. As the Indians chased the train, they began to gain on it and shoot arrows into the cars, wounding and killing many passengers. The people were desperate. Then, a conductor went to the coal car to help some men who were shoveling coal into the engine's furnace as fast as they could. The more they shoveled, the hotter the fire became and the more steam pressure the engine produced. In a few minutes, the train gained speed and began to leave the Indians behind.

After that old movie went through my mind, the Lord spoke to me and said:

"Roxanne, that is a principle I want you to emphasize to people as you speak on the growth of faith: Just as feeding coal into the train's firebox will produce more steam and result in the action of increased speed, so in the spiritual realm the same thing happens regarding production of faith in an increased way. The more a Christian shovels My Word into himself, the more faith is produced.

"Faith is like a force or pressure which increases in a Christian's life; and that faith, when strong enough, will issue in actions. In other words, shoveling more coal into the engine's firebox increases steam pressure which, in turn, moves the wheels of the train. In a parallel way, in the spiritual realm, *shoveling more of My Word into your spirit produces an increase in the force of faith which results in corresponding actions or faith-filled actions in line with My Word.*"

Jesus continued, "So many of My people are looking for the results or actions of faith too soon. They are trying to go outside and move the train by pushing it down the tracks. That's not the way it's done. That train was made a certain way, and that's the only way it runs. If you want a steam engine to run, you've got to feed it coal and wait while the engine builds up steam pressure. Then, when the train gets moving, you still have to consistently feed coal into it. Faith has similar principles.''

I really understood then what Jesus wanted me to emphasize to people about increasing their faith. *Faith is produced and increased by feeding on God's Word and acting on it*. In time, more of the **FORCE OF FAITH** will be generated within us, having the power to move great obstacles.

The Word of God is the coal of Faith's Steam Engine. If you don't put any of God's Word into your system, you won't get any faith power out. So shovel it in daily! Then faith will be produced just as surely as steam is produced in a steam engine after coal is used for fuel.

God's Word Is Faith's Fuel

Sometimes I am absolutely amazed at how strong the spiritual part of us, *the inner man,* can become if we will just feed him with God's Word. You will be surprised at what he will say and do when you get him filled up or fired up with God's Word. **The by-products of that Word — the faith, life, and power of God — will begin to be manifested in your life.**

You will soon begin to see that faith isn't the only thing you have received, for **the law of God's growth** will take over in **every** area of your life. You will find yourself growing:

in the knowledge of God (Col. 1:10).

in love (1 Thess. 3:12).

in the fruits of righteousness (2 Cor. 9:10).

in His grace (2 Pet. 3:18).

All for His glory!

Appendix

Faith Builders

The following are some scriptures that tell you what God has done for you in Jesus Christ and who you are in Him.

Confess these *continuously* and *consistently* until your confession brings into your life the possession of what legally belongs to you.

WHO GOD SAYS YOU ARE IN CHRIST
IN CHRIST:
Romans 3:24
Being justified freely by his grace through the redemption that is in Christ Jesus.

Romans 8:1
There is therefore now no condemnation to them which are in Christ Jesus.

Romans 8:2
For the law of the Spirit of life in Christ Jesus hath made me free from the law of sin and death.

Romans 12:5
So we, being many, are one body in Christ, and every one members one of another.

1 Corinthians 1:2
Unto the church of God which is at Corinth, to them that are sanctified in Christ Jesus, called to be saints, with all that in every place call upon the name of Jesus Christ our Lord, both theirs and ours.

1 Corinthians 1:30
But of him are ye in Christ Jesus, who of God is made unto us wisdom, and righteousness, and sanctification, and redemption.

1 Corinthians 15:22
For as in Adam all die, even so in Christ shall all be made alive.

2 Corinthians 1:21
Now he which stablisheth us with you in Christ, and hath anointed us, is God.

2 Corinthians 2:14
Now thanks be unto God, which always causeth us to triumph in Christ, and maketh manifest the savour of his knowledge by us in every place.

2 Corinthians 3:14
But their minds were blinded: for until this day remaineth the same veil untaken away in the reading of the old testament; which veil is done away in Christ.

2 Corinthians 5:17
Therefore if any man be in Christ, he is a new creature: old things are passed away; behold, all things are become new.

2 Corinthians 5:19
To wit, that God was in Christ, reconciling the world unto himself, not imputing their trespasses unto them; and hath committed unto us the word of reconciliation.

Galatians 2:4
And that because of false brethren unawares brought in, who came in privily to spy out our liberty which we have in Christ Jesus, that they might bring us into bondage.

Galatians 3:26
For ye are all the children of God by faith in Christ Jesus.

Galatians 3:28
There is neither Jew nor Greek, there is neither bond nor free, there is neither male nor female: for ye are all one in Christ Jesus.

Galatians 5:6
For in Jesus Christ neither circumcision availeth any thing, nor uncircumcision; but faith which worketh by love.

Galatians 6:15
For in Christ Jesus neither circumcision availeth any thing, nor uncircumcision, but a new creature.

Ephesians 1:3
Blessed be the God and Father of our Lord Jesus Christ, who hath blessed us with all spiritual blessings in heavenly places in Christ.

Ephesians 1:10
That in the dispensation of the fulness of times he might gather together in one all things in Christ, both which are in heaven, and which are on earth; even in him.

Ephesians 2:6
And hath raised us up together, and made us sit together in heavenly places in Christ Jesus.

Ephesians 2:10
For we are his workmanship, created in Christ Jesus unto good works, which God hath before ordained that we should walk in them.

Ephesians 2:13
But now in Christ Jesus ye who sometimes were far off are made nigh by the blood of Christ.

Ephesians 3:6
That the Gentiles should be fellowheirs, and of the same body, and partakers of his promise in Christ by the gospel.

Philippians 3:13, 14
Brethren, I count not myself to have apprehended: but this one thing I do, forgetting those things which are behind, and reaching forth unto those things which are before, I press toward the mark for the prize of the high calling of God in Christ Jesus.

Colossians 1:28
Whom we preach, warning every man, and teaching every man in all wisdom; that we may present every man perfect in Christ Jesus.

1 Thessalonians 4:16
For the Lord himself shall descend from heaven with a shout, with the voice of the archangel, and with the trump of God: and the dead in Christ shall rise first.

1 Thessalonians 5:18
In every thing give thanks: for this is the will of God in Christ Jesus concerning you.

1 Timothy 1:14
And the grace of our Lord was exceeding abundant with faith and love which is in Christ Jesus.

2 Timothy 1:9
Who hath saved us, and called us with an holy calling, not according to our works, but according to his own purpose and grace, which was given us in Christ Jesus before the world began.

2 Timothy 1:13
Hold fast the form of sound words, which thou hast heard of me, in faith and love which is in Christ Jesus.

2 Timothy 2:1
Thou therefore, my son, be strong in the grace that is in Christ Jesus.

2 Timothy 2:10
Therefore I endure all things for the elect's sakes, that they may also obtain the salvation which is in Christ Jesus with eternal glory.

2 Timothy 3:15
And that from a child thou hast known the holy scriptures, which are able to make thee wise unto salvation through faith which is in Christ Jesus.

Philemon 1:6
That the communication of thy faith may become effectual by the acknowledging of every good thing which is in you in Christ Jesus.

2 Peter 1:8
For if these things be in you, and abound, they make you that ye shall neither be barren nor unfruitful in the knowledge of our Lord Jesus Christ.

2 John 1:9
Whosoever transgresseth, and abideth not in the doctrine of Christ, hath not God. He that abideth in the doctrine of Christ, he hath both the Father and the Son.

BY CHRIST:

Romans 3:22
Even the righteousness of God which is by faith of Jesus Christ unto all and upon all them that believe: for there is no difference.

Romans 5:15
But not as the offence, so also is the free gift. For if through the offence of one many be dead, much more the grace of God, and the gift by grace, which is by one man, Jesus Christ, hath abounded unto many.

Romans 5:17-19
For if by one man's offence death reigned by one; much more they which receive abundance of grace and of the gift of righteousness shall reign in life by one, Jesus Christ.

Therefore as by the offence of one judgment came upon all men to condemnation; even so by the righteousness of one the free gift came upon all men unto justification of life.

For as by one man's disobedience many were made sinners, so by the obedience of one shall many be made righteous.

Romans 7:4
Wherefore, my brethren, ye also are become dead to the law by the body of Christ; that ye should be married to another, even to him who is raised from the dead, that we should bring forth fruit unto God.

1 Corinthians 1:4
I thank my God always on your behalf, for the grace of God which is given you by Jesus Christ.

2 Corinthians 5:18
And all things are of God, who hath reconciled us to himself by Jesus Christ, and hath given to us the ministry of reconciliation.

Galatians 2:16
Knowing that a man is not justified by the works of the law, but by the faith of Jesus Christ, even we have believed in Jesus Christ, that we might be justified by the faith of Christ, and not by the works of the law: for by the works of the law shall no flesh be justified.

Ephesians 1:5
Having predestinated us unto the adoption of children by Jesus Christ to himself, according to the good pleasure of His will.

Philippians 1:11
Being filled with the fruits of righteousness, which are by Jesus Christ, unto the glory and praise of God.

Philippians 4:19
But my God shall supply all your need according to his riches in glory by Christ Jesus.

1 Peter 1:3
Blessed be the God and Father of our Lord Jesus Christ, which according to his abundant mercy hath begotten us again unto a lively hope by the resurrection of Jesus Christ from the dead.

1 Peter 2:5
Ye also, as lively stones, are built up a spiritual house, an holy priesthood, to offer up spiritual sacrifices, acceptable to God by Jesus Christ.

1 Peter 5:10
But the God of all grace, who hath called us unto his eternal glory by Christ Jesus, after that ye have suffered a while, make you perfect, stablish, strengthen, settle you.

OF CHRIST:

2 Corinthians 2:15
For we are unto God a sweet savour of Christ, in them that are saved, and in them that perish.

Philippians 3:12
Not as though I had already attained, either were already perfect: but I follow after, if that I may apprehend that for which also I am apprehended of Christ Jesus.

Colossians 2:17
Which are a shadow of things to come; but the body is of Christ.

Colossians 3:24
Knowing that of the Lord ye shall receive the reward of the inheritance: for ye serve the Lord Christ.

THROUGH CHRIST:

Romans 5:1
Therefore being justified by faith, we have peace with God through our Lord Jesus Christ.

Romans 5:11
And not only so, but we also joy in God through our Lord Jesus Christ, by whom we have now received the atonement.

Romans 6:11
Likewise reckon ye also yourselves to be dead indeed unto sin, but alive unto God through Jesus Christ our Lord.

Romans 6:23
For the wages of sin is death; but the gift of God is eternal life through Jesus Christ our Lord.

1 Corinthians 15:57
But thanks be to God, which giveth us the victory through our Lord Jesus Christ.

Galatians 3:13, 14
Christ hath redeemed us from the curse of the law, being made a curse for us: for it is written, Cursed is every one that hangeth on a tree: That the blessing of Abraham might come on the Gentiles through Jesus Christ; that we might receive the promise of the Spirit through faith.

Galatians 4:7
Wherefore thou art no more a servant, but a son; and if a son, then an heir of God through Christ.

Ephesians 2:7
That in the ages to come he might shew the exceeding riches of his grace in his kindness toward us through Christ Jesus.

Philippians 4:6, 7
Be careful for nothing; but in every thing by prayer and supplication with thanksgiving let your requests be made known unto God.

And the peace of God, which passeth all understanding, shall keep your hearts and minds through Christ Jesus.

Philippians 4:13
I can do all things through Christ which strengtheneth me.

Hebrews 10:10
By the which will we are sanctified through the offering of the body of Jesus Christ once for all.

Hebrews 13:20, 21
Now the God of peace, that brought again from the dead our Lord Jesus, that great shepherd of the sheep, through the blood of the everlasting covenant,

Make you perfect in every good work to do his will, working in you that which is well-pleasing in his sight, through Jesus Christ; to whom be glory for ever and ever. Amen.

WITH CHRIST:

Romans 5:8
But God commendeth his love toward us, in that, while we were yet sinners, Christ died for us.

Galatians 2:20
I am crucified with Christ: nevertheless I live; yet not I, but Christ liveth in me: and the life which I now live in the flesh I live by the faith of the Son of God, who loved me, and gave himself for me.

Ephesians 2:5
Even when we were dead in sins, hath quickened us together with Christ, (by grace ye are saved;).

Colossians 2:20
Wherefore if ye be dead with Christ from the rudiments of the world, why, as though living in the world, are ye subject to ordinances.

Colossians 3:1
If ye then be risen with Christ, seek those things which are above, where Christ sitteth on the right hand of God.

Colossians 3:3
For ye are dead, and your life is hid with Christ in God.

IN HIM:

Acts 17:28
For in him we live, and move, and have our being; as certain also of your own poets have said, For we are also his offspring.

John 1:4
In him was life; and the life was the light of men.

John 3:15, 16
That whosoever believeth in him should not perish, but have eternal life.

For God so loved the world, that he gave his only begotten Son, that whosoever believeth in him should not perish, but have everlasting life.

2 Corinthians 1:20
For all the promises of God in him are yea, and in him Amen, unto the glory of God by us.

2 Corinthians 5:21
For he hath made him to be sin for us, who knew no sin; that we might be made the righteousness of God in him.

Ephesians 1:4
According as he hath chosen us in him before the foundation of the world, that we should be holy and without blame before him in love.

Ephesians 1:10
That in the dispensation of the fulness of times he might gather together in one all things in Christ, both which are in heaven, and which are on earth; even in him.

Philippians 3:9
And be found in him, not having mine own right-eousness, which is of the law, but that which is through the faith of Christ, the righteousness which is of God by faith.

Colossians 2:6
As ye have therefore received Christ Jesus the Lord, so walk ye in him.

Colossians 2:7
Rooted and built up in him, and stablished in the faith, as ye have been taught, abounding therein with thanksgiving.

Colossians 2:10
And ye are complete in him, which is the head of all principality and power.

1 John 2:5
But whoso keepeth his word, in him verily is the love of God perfected: hereby know we that we are in him.

1 John 2:6
He that saith he abideth in him ought himself also so to walk, even as he walked.

1 John 2:8
Again, a new commandment I write unto you, which thing is true in him and in you: because the darkness is past, and the true light now shineth.

1 John 2:27
But the anointing which ye have received of him abideth in you, and ye need not that any man teach you: but as the same anointing teacheth you of all things, and is truth, and is no lie, and even as it hath taught you, ye shall abide in him.

1 John 2:28
And now, little children, abide in him; that, when he shall appear, we may have confidence, and not be ashamed before him at his coming.

1 John 3:3
And every man that hath this hope in him purifieth himself, even as he is pure.

1 John 3:5
And ye know that he was manifested to take away our sins; and in him is no sin.

1 John 3:6
Whosoever abideth in him sinneth not: whosoever sinneth hath not seen him, neither known him.

1 John 3:24
And he that keepeth his commandments dwelleth in him, and he in him. And hereby we know that he abideth in us, by the Spirit which he hath given us.

1 John 4:13
Hereby know we that we dwell in him, and he in us, because he hath given us of his Spirit.

1 John 5:14, 15
And this is the confidence that we have in him, that, if we ask any thing according to his will, he heareth us:

And if we know that He hear us, whatsoever we ask, we know that we have the petitions that we desired of him.

1 John 5:20
And we know that the Son of God is come, and hath given us an understanding, that we may know him

that is true, and we are in him that is true, even in his Son Jesus Christ. This is the true God, and eternal life.

BY HIM:

1 Corinthians 1:5
That in every thing ye are enriched by him, in all utterance, and in all knowledge.

1 Corinthians 8:6
But to us there is but one God, the Father, of whom are all things, and we in him; and one Lord Jesus Christ, by whom are all things, and we by him.

Colossians 1:16
For by him were all things created, that are in heaven, and that are in earth, visible and invisible, whether they be thrones, or dominions, or principalities, or powers: all things were created by him, and for him.

Colossians 1:17
And he is before all things, and by him all things consist.

Colossians 1:20
And, having made peace through the blood of his cross, by Him to reconcile all things unto himself; by him, I say, whether they be things in earth, or things in heaven.

Colossians 3:17
And whatsoever ye do in word or deed, do all in the name of the Lord Jesus, giving thanks to God and the Father by him.

Hebrews 7:25
Wherefore he is able also to save them to the uttermost that come unto God by him, seeing he ever liveth to make intercession for them.

Hebrews 13:15
By him therefore let us offer the sacrifice of praise to God continually, that is, the fruit of our lips giving thanks to his name.

1 Peter 1:21
Who by him do believe in God, that raised him up from the dead, and gave him glory; that your faith and hope might be in God.

OF HIM:

1 John 1:5
This then is the message which we have heard of him, and declare unto you, that God is light, and in him is no darkness at all.

1 John 2:27
But the anointing which ye have received of him abideth in you, and ye need not that any man teach you: but as the same anointing teacheth you of all things, and is truth, and is no lie, and even as it hath taught you, ye shall abide in him.

THROUGH HIM:

John 3:17
For God sent not his Son into the world to condemn the world; but that the world through him might be saved.

Romans 5:9
Much more then, being now justified by his blood, we shall be saved from wrath through him.

Romans 8:37
Nay, in all these things we are more than conquerors through him that loved us.

1 John 4:9
In this was manifested the love of God toward us, because that God sent his only begotten Son into the world, that we might live through him.

WITH HIM:

Romans 6:4
Therefore we are buried with him by baptism into death: that like as Christ was raised up from the dead by the glory of the Father, even so we also should walk in newness of life.

Romans 6:6
Knowing this, that our old man is crucified with him, that the body of sin might be destroyed, that henceforth we should not serve sin.

Romans 6:8
Now if we be dead with Christ, we believe that we shall also live with him.

Romans 8:32
He that spared not his own Son, but delivered him up for us all, how shall he not with him also freely give us all things?

2 Corinthians 13:4
For though he was crucified through weakness, yet he liveth by the power of God. For we also are weak in him, but we shall live with him by the power of God toward you.

Colossians 2:12
Buried with him in baptism, wherein also ye are risen with him through the faith of the operation of God, who hath raised him from the dead.

Colossians 2:13-15
And you, being dead in your sins and the uncircumcision of your flesh, hath he quickened together with him, having forgiven you all trespasses;

Blotting out the handwriting of ordinances that was against us, which was contrary to us, and took it out of the way, nailing it to his cross;

And having spoiled principalities and powers, he made a shew of them openly, triumphing over them in it.

Colossians 3:4
When Christ, who is our life, shall appear, then shall ye also appear with him in glory.

2 Timothy 2:11, 12
It is a faithful saying: For if we be dead with him, we shall also live with him:

If we suffer, we shall also reign with him: if we deny him, he also will deny us.

IN WHOM:

Ephesians 1:7
In whom we have redemption through his blood, the forgiveness of sins, according to the riches of his grace.

Ephesians 1:11
In whom also we have obtained an inheritance, being predestinated according to the purpose of him who worketh all things after the counsel of his own will.

Ephesians 1:13
In whom ye also trusted, after that ye heard the word of truth, the gospel of your salvation: in whom also after that ye believed, ye were sealed with that Holy Spirit of promise.

Ephesians 2:21
In whom all the building fitly framed together groweth unto an holy temple in the Lord.

Ephesians 2:22
In whom ye also are builded together for an habitation of God through the Spirit.

Ephesians 3:12
In whom we have boldness and access with confidence by the faith of him.

Colossians 1:14
In whom we have redemption through his blood, even the forgiveness of sins.

Colossians 2:3
In whom are hid all the treasures of wisdom and knowledge.

Colossians 2:11
*In whom also ye are circumcised with the cir-
cumcision made without hands, in putting off the
body of the sins of the flesh by the circumcision of
Christ.*

1 Peter 1:8
*Whom having not seen, ye love; in whom, though
now ye see him not, yet believing, ye rejoice with joy
unspeakable and full of glory.*

BY WHOM:

Romans 5:2
*By whom also we have access by faith into this grace
wherein we stand, and rejoice in hope of the glory of
God.*

Romans 5:11
*And not only so, but we also joy in God through our
Lord Jesus Christ, by whom we have now received the
atonement.*

Galatians 6:14
*But God forbid that I should glory, save in the cross
of our Lord Jesus Christ, by whom the world is
crucified unto me, and I unto the world.*

FROM WHOM:

Ephesians 4:16
*From whom the whole body fitly joined together and
compacted by that which every joint supplieth,
according to the effectual working in the measure
of every part, maketh increase of the body unto the
edifying of itself in love.*

Colossians 2:19

And not holding the Head, from which all the body by joints and bands having nourishment ministered, and knit together, increaseth with the increase of God.

BY ME:

John 6:57

As the living Father hath sent me, and I live by the Father: so he that eateth me, even he shall live by me.

John 14:6

Jesus saith unto him, I am the way, the truth, and the life: no man cometh unto the Father, but by me.

IN ME:

John 6:56

He that eateth my flesh, and drinketh my blood, dwelleth in me, and I in him.

John 14:20

And at that day ye shall know that I am in my Father, and ye in me, and I in you.

John 15:4, 5

Abide in me, and I in you. As the branch cannot bear fruit of itself, except it abide in the vine; no more can ye, except ye abide in me.

I am the vine, ye are the branches. He that abideth in me, and I in him, the same bringeth forth much fruit: for without me ye can do nothing.

John 15:7, 8

If ye abide in me, and my words abide in you, ye shall ask what ye will, and it shall be done unto you.

Herein is my Father glorified, that ye bear much fruit; so shall ye be my disciples.

John 16:33
These things I have spoken unto you, that in me ye might have peace. In the world ye shall have tribulation: but be of good cheer; I have overcome the world.

BY HIMSELF:

Hebrews 1:3
Who being the brightness of his glory, and the express image of his person, and upholding all things by the word of his power, when he had by himself purged our sins, sat down on the right hand of the Majesty on high.

Hebrews 9:26
For then must he often have suffered since the foundation of the world: but now once in the end of the world hath he appeared to put away sin by the sacrifice of himself.

IN THE LORD:

Ephesians 5:8
For ye were sometimes darkness, but now are ye light in the Lord: walk as children of light.

Ephesians 6:10
Finally, my brethren, be strong in the Lord, and in the power of his might.

IN THE BELOVED:

Ephesians 1:6
To the praise of the glory of his grace, wherein he hath made us accepted in the beloved.

BY HIS BLOOD:

Hebrews 9:11, 12
But Christ being come an high priest of good things to come, by a greater and more perfect tabernacle, not made with hands, that is to say, not of this building;

Neither by the blood of goats and calves, but by his own blood he entered in once into the holy place, having obtained eternal redemption for us.

Hebrews 9:14, 15
How much more shall the blood of Christ, who through the eternal Spirit offered himself without spot to God, purge your conscience from dead works to serve the living God?

And for this cause he is mediator of the new testament, that by means of death, for the redemption of the transgressions that were under the first testament, they which are called might receive the promise of eternal inheritance.

Hebrews 10:19, 20
Having therefore, brethren, boldness to enter into the holiest by the blood of Jesus,

By a new and living way, which he hath consecrated for us, through the veil, that is to say, his flesh.

1 John 1:7

But if we walk in the light, as he is in the light, we have fellowship one with another, and the blood of Jesus Christ his Son cleanseth us from all sin.

IN MY LOVE:

John 15:9

As the Father hath loved me, so have I loved you: continue ye in my love.

IN HIS NAME:

Matthew 18:20

For where two or three are gathered together in my name, there am I in the midst of them.

Mark 16:17, 18

And these signs shall follow them that believe; In my name shall they cast out devils; they shall speak with new tongues;

They shall take up serpents; and if they drink any deadly thing, it shall not hurt them; they shall lay hands on the sick, and they shall recover.

John 14:13, 14

And whatsoever ye shall ask in my name, that will I do, that the Father may be glorified in the Son.

If ye shall ask any thing in my name, I will do it.

John 16:23, 24

And in that day ye shall ask me nothing. Verily, verily, I say unto you, Whatsoever ye shall ask the Father in my name, he will give it you.

Hitherto have ye asked nothing in my name: ask, and ye shall receive, that your joy may be full.

1 Corinthians 6:11
And such were some of you: but ye are washed, but ye are sanctified, but ye are justified in the name of the Lord Jesus, and by the Spirit of our God.

The Bible contains many more verses describing who you are or what you have in Christ. However, these verses do not use the specific phrases such as, *in Him, in Christ, of Christ,* etc. Therefore, you have to search the Scriptures for yourself and find out your inheritance in Christ.

Several of these verses are listed as follows:

Matthew 8:17	Hebrews 2:9-11
Mark 11:23, 24	Hebrews 13:8
Luke 10:19	James 4:7
John 10:10	1 Peter 2:9
Galatians 5:1	1 Peter 5:7
Philippians 2:5	1 John 1:9
Philippians 2:13	1 John 4:4
Colossians 1:13	1 John 5:11, 12

As an anointed minister of the Gospel, Roxanne Brant conducts miracle services and crusades throughout the United States, Canada, and other parts of the world.

Her educational background includes studies at *Harvard Divinity School, Boston University School of Theology,* and *Gordon Divinity School* from which she received a *Master of Divinity* degree.

If you are interested in having a crusade or a teaching conference in your church or area, or if you desire a list of Miss Brant's cassette tapes, please contact:

Coordinator of Ministries
Roxanne Brant Crusades, Inc.
P. O. Box 1000
O'Brien, FL 32071
(904) 935-0948

MINISTERING TO THE LORD

In this book, Roxanne Brant shares the truths that have revolutionized her life and ministry, as well as the lives and ministries of thousands. It all started with a vision of Jesus during a worship service.

Read it. It will change *your* life, too!

$3.50 per copy
(includes mailing costs)

Write for information on quantity discounts.

HOW TO TEST PROPHECY, PREACHING AND GUIDANCE

$5.50 per copy
216 pages

In this book, Rev. Brant teaches you HOW TO TEST PROPHECY, PREACHING AND GUIDANCE. You will discover the process and results of testing spiritual phenomena. You will be able to distinguish the genuine from the counterfeit by applying Scriptural tests to all ministry.

Rev. Brant addresses questions such as: Is the phenomenon or ministry Scriptural? Does it glorify Jesus Christ? Is there an inward witness to it? Does it produce liberty instead of bondage? Is the fruit good? And if it is prophecy, does it come to pass?

**EVERY CHRISTIAN NEEDS TO READ
THIS BOOK!**

CLIP OUT ORDER FORM

NUMBER	TITLE	PRICE
_____	How to Test Prophecy, Preaching and Guidance	$5.50
_____	The Growing Power of Faith	$3.50
_____	Ministering to the Lord	$3.50
_____	Guidance [6-Cassette Series with Folder]	$25.00
_____	Recent Angelic Visitations	$1.25

PLUS
MANY OTHER BOOKS
AND CASSETTES

_____	Put me on your mailing list.
$ _____	SUBTOTAL
$ _____	ADD $1.00 (POSTAGE)
$ _____	TOTAL ENCLOSED
	MINIMUM ORDER — $4.00

Order from and make checks payable to:

Roxanne Brant Crusades
P.O. Box 1000
O'Brien, Florida 32071

Send Materials to (PLEASE PRINT):

NAME _____

ADDRESS _____

CITY _____

STATE _____ ZIP CODE _____

(Standard trade discounts available to bookstores.)